Buying Classical Records Is Not Easy, which is why I've written this simple guide.

Whether you are a new or experienced listener, the problem is the same: How do you discover, out of the hundreds of composers and thousands of works available, what you want? You can't listen to records in the store. Unless you have a lot of extra time and money to waste you don't want to buy randomly. Record reviews are only helpful after you know the specific piece you want. Music histories are only helpful after you know the music.

THE AIM OF THIS GUIDE is to help you solve this problem—to help you discover and explore as quickly and easily as possible the rich world of classical music.

Munford's Simple Guide to Classical Music

by

Gregory Allen Munford

JEMCO Enterprises
P.O. Box 422
Wilmette, Illinois 60091

ISBN: 0-9602760-0-9   L.C. 79-88204

The Purpose of This Guide

Classical records are not easy to buy, as anyone who has ever tried surely knows. For while there are literally thousands of recorded works to choose from, they are impossible to sample, to thumb through, to "shop for." The record is a closed book which cannot be opened until paid for.

If you're interested in classical music—whether you're exploring it for the first time or expanding what knowledge you have—this creates a problem: How do you begin to explore the repertoire, how do you know which pieces you want to hear, how do you know what you want to buy?

The classical repertoire, after all, is not easy to get to know. Even if you regularly attend classical concerts (including orchestral, chamber and choral concerts, solo recitals *and* the opera); or listen extensively to the local classical radio station, you're still going to get just a taste of what's available. And an imbalanced one at that.

The fact is that the world of classical music is so immense and complex that without some kind of help, you are simply at a loss. Whether you are a new or experienced listener, you must proceed blindly, buying at random, relying on hunches, sticking to what you chance to hear or someone happens to recommend.

What is needed is a simple, straightforward map of the classical music repertoire which would help the newcomer get started and which would assist the experienced listener in seeking out new areas according to his own tastes. That is the purpose of this guide.

The backbone of this guide is a series of lists containing over 400 composers, nearly 1000 works and over 200 recommended recordings which are structured, indexed and annotated in such a way as to function as any good tour map does—distinguishing the highways from the back roads, singling out high points, and generally providing a sense of the lay of the land. And, of course, it shows how to get from one point to another, whether you want a broad overview or to explore a single area in depth; whether you want to stick to main highways and see only the most treasured and famous sights, or explore the lesser known, more specialized out of the way areas. Thus, as with any map, this guide neither tells you where to go nor dictates what you should or must like. It is simply a tool, the main purpose of which is to help you find what you want.

Special thanks to Susan Gross for her invaluable advice and assistance.

Cover illustration by John Youssi.

Design and typography by Siemens Communication Graphics.

Table of Contents

Use and organization of the guide

How to Use This Guide

As the title suggests, this guide is very simple to use. To ensure maximum use, however, please take just a few moments to read through these brief directions, and then skim through the rest of the guide in order to familiarize yourself with its contents and layout.

The bulk of this guide consists of . . .

INTRODUCTORY LIST (p. 9)
- 15 composers and 34 works, designed to provide points of introduction for the new listener.

CORE COMPOSERS LIST (p. 12)
- 37 composers, designed to provide focal points or touchstones across the broad sweep of classical music.

100 KEY MASTERWORKS with recommended recordings. (p. 13)
- Representing a cross section of some of the "essential" works of the repertoire.

COMPLETE LIST (p. 26)
- All composers and works in this guide.
- Composers grouped into the chronologically arranged six main stylistic periods (Medieval, Renaissance, Baroque, Classical, Romantic, Modern) and their sub-groups.
- Main composers of each group listed (in chronological order) first, in bold type, followed by the lesser composers of that group.
- Check marks next to works suggested as starting points for that composer.

COMMENTARY ON STYLISTIC PERIODS (p. 88)
- Discusses each of the stylistic periods and their sub-groups on the Complete List.

INDEX OF COMPOSERS (p. 128)
- Arranges all of the composers in this guide alphabetically and locates them throughout the guide.

DISCOVERING CLASSICAL MUSIC

ARE YOU A NEW LISTENER? Do you recognize just a few of the names of the most famous composers? And perhaps a scattering of the most well-known pieces? Or maybe none at all? If so, there are several ways you can use this guide to help you discover classical music. (For advice on buying records see p. 109).

Using the Introductory List. This list of 34 works and 15 composers ranging from the Medieval through the Modern period is designed to provide you with points of introduction to the six major stylistic periods of music (Medieval, Renaissance, Baroque, Classical, Romantic, Modern). The "Golden Age" of classical music is said to run from the end of the Baroque period (c. 1700) to the beginning of the Modern (c. 1900). Most of the great masterpieces of music were written within this span of time, making this a likely place to begin. I would suggest, however, listening to just one or two pieces from each main stylistic period in order to get a general overview of the scope of classical music. Skimming through the Stylistic Period Commentary may be of help in deciding where you will want to begin.

Using the Core Composers List. You might want to run down this list of 37 composers and try sampling a few of the works of some of the more familiar names. This list contains only composers' names, so you'll have to turn to the Complete List for suggested pieces. Works on the Complete List with a checkmark next to them are suggested starting points for that composer.

The 100 Key Masterworks. You might want to begin by picking a few pieces from this cross section of "essential" works of the classical repertoire.

Starting with a composer you know. Another way to proceed is to look up in the index a composer you know or have heard of and try listening to some of the pieces suggested on the Complete List.

Using the Light Classics List. Still another way to begin discovering classical music is to choose some works from the Light Classics list on p. 24. These tuneful, colorful works are generally considered easily accessible to the newcomer to classical music. They are all orchestral works from the Romantic school.

After you have made an initial start and have discovered a composer or an area or style of music that you like or that is interesting to you, you are ready to begin exploring further.

EXPLORING CLASSICAL MUSIC

ARE YOU AN EXPERIENCED LISTENER? Do you have some sense of what you like? Are you fairly well acquainted with a few composers or periods of classical music, but want to increase your tastes and knowledge? If so, this guide can be used in a variety of ways.

Expanding from what you know. This guide is organized in such a way as to help you build on what familiarity you have of classical music, to use that familiarity as a home base from which to expand your knowledge. It does this by grouping the composers and works on the complete list into stylistically homogeneous categories (called Stylistic Periods) of gradually increasing scope and size which enables you to place the composers and works you know into context with other composers whose works are in a similar style. Thus, for example, if you like Bach's music, the guide shows that the music of Vivaldi or Handel should perhaps also be explored. Or if you like Schubert songs, perhaps you would be interested in those of Schumann or Brahms as well. A complete Outline of Stylistic Periods and their sub-groups may be found preceeding the Commentary on p. 85. The Map of Stylistic Periods on p. 87 shows at a glance the general relationships between these groups and subgroups, while the Commentary discusses briefly the nature of the groups and the relationships between them.

Discovering new areas. Few people, of course, no matter how knowledgeable they are about some areas of classical music, are equally familiar with the full scope of the repertory. Even if you are an expert in one or two areas, it can always be exciting to discover "new" music and styles. One way to do this is to play the part of the novice and follow the advice given above for the new listener, concentrating, of course, on those areas unfamiliar to you.

Exploring a single area in depth. The large number of composers included in this guide combined with the method of organization used—grouping them into stylistically homogeneous categories—allows you to explore a single stylistic area in depth. On the complete list, the most important composers of any stylistic period or sub-group thereof are presented, within their group, first, and appear in bold print. They are followed by the lesser composers of the group. It can be a fascinating experience to hear the contrast not only between the great masters of a single period, such as Bach and Handel, but between them and their lesser though more typical contemporaries as well.

Lists of composers

Introductory List
Core Composers List
100 Key Masterworks
Light Classics
Complete List

Introductory List

This list is designed to provide points of introduction to the six major stylistic periods of music.

MEDIEVAL 500-1420
see also page 88
Guillaume de Machaut c. 1300-1377
—Chansons (for solo voice with instrumental accompaniment)

RENAISSANCE c. 1420-1474
see also page 89

Guillaume Dufay c. 1420-1474

—Chansons (for solo voice with instrumental accompaniment)
—Mass: Se la face ay pale (for chorus with instruments)

Josquin des Prez c. 1440/50-1521

—Mass: Pange lingua (for a capella chorus)
—Motet: Miserere mei Deus; Planxit autem David (for a cappella chorus)

BAROQUE 1600-1750
see also page 91

Johann Sebastian Bach 1685-1750

Vocal
—Cantata: #4, Christ lag in Todesbanden (for chorus, orchestra and solo voices)
—Oratorio: Passion according to St. Matthew (for chorus, orchestra and solo voices)

Instrumental
—Brandenburg concertos (6) (for small orchestra)
—Well Tempered Clavier, Book I (for harpsichord)

George Frideric Handel 1685-1759

Vocal
—Oratorio: Messiah (for orchestra, chorus and solo voices)
Instrumental
—Water Music (for orchestra)

see also
page 94
CLASSICAL 1725-1800

Wolfgang Amadeus Mozart 1756-1791

Vocal
—opera: Marriage of Figaro
Instrumental
—Symphony #40 in G minor
—Piano Concerto K. 467 in C (for piano and orchestra)

Ludwig van Beethoven 1770-1827

—Symphony #5 and #6
—Piano sonata #8, Op. 13 (Pathetique) (for piano solo)
—String Quartet Op. 131 in C# minor

see also
page 97
ROMANTIC 1800-1900

Franz Schubert 1797-1828

—Die Wintereise (song cycle for solo voice and piano)

Frédéric Chopin 1810-1849

—4 Scherzos (for piano solo); 24 Preludes, Op. 28 (for piano solo)

Richard Wagner 1813-1883

Vocal
—opera: Tristan und Isolde
Instrumental
—Prelude to Tristan und Isolde (for orchestra); Prelude to Der Meistersinger (for orchestra)

Guiseppe Verdi 1813-1901

—opera: La Traviata

Johannes Brahms 1833-1897

—Symphony #4
—Six Pieces for Piano, Op. 118

Pitor Ilyitch Tchaikovsky 1840-1893
—The Nutcracker Ballet (for orchestra)
—Symphony #6 (Pathetique)

MODERN 1900-Present

see also
page 101

Arnold Schoenberg 1874-1951

—Pierrot Lunaire (for solo voice and instruments)
—Three Piano Pieces, Op. 11

Igor Stravinsky 1882-1971

—Le Sacre de prentemps (The Rite of Spring) (for orchestra)
—Dumbarton Oaks (for small orchestra)

Core Composers

This list is designed to provide focal points or touchstones across the broad sweep of classical music. The composers on this list are designated on the Complete List with a star (★).

MEDIEVAL

Guillaume de Machaut

RENAISSANCE

Guillaume Dufay
Johannes Ockeghem
Heinrich Isaac
Josquin Des Prez
Pierluigi da Palestrina
William Byrd

BAROQUE

Claudio Monteverdi
Antonio Vivaldi
Johann Sebastian Bach
George Frideric Handel
Jean-Phillipe Rameau

CLASSICAL

Franz Joseph Haydn
Wolfgang Amadeus Mozart
Ludwig Van Beethoven

ROMANTIC

Franz Schubert
Gaetano Donizetti
Hector Berlioz
Felix Mendelssohn
Frédéric Chopin
Robert Schumann
Franz Liszt
Richard Wagner
Guiseppe Verdi
Anton Bruckner
Johannes Brahms
Pitor Tchaikovsky
Gustav Mahler
Claude Debussy
Giacomo Puccini
Richard Strauss

MODERN

Arnold Schoenberg
Béla Bartók
Igor Stravinsky
Edgard Varèse
Alban Berg
Paul Hindemith

100 Key Masterworks

with recommended recordings

This list contains a cross section of some of the "essential" works of the classical repertoire. The recordings recommended are purely a reflection of my own personal taste and in no way represent the only good recordings of these pieces available. (For general advice on buying records, see p. 109).

J. S. Bach

Brandenburg Concertos.
  2 Telefunken 2635043, Harnoncourt, Con. Mus.
  2 ABC 67020, Leonhardt, Leonhardt Consort.

Cantata # 4, Christ lag in Todesbanden.
  2 Telefunken 2635027, Harnoncourt, Con. Mus.

Mass in B min.
  3 Telefunken 3635019, Harnoncourt, Con. Mus.
  3 Deutsche Grammaphon ARC-2710001, Richter.
  (excerpts of above: Deutsche Grammaphon 136300)
  3 Philips 6769002, Marriner, St. Martin's.

Passion according to St. John.
  3 Deutsche Grammaphon ARC-270002, Richter, Munich Bach Orchestra.

Passion according to St. Matthew.
  4 Telefunken 4635047, Harnoncourt, Con. Mus.
  4 Deutsche Grammaphon ARC-2712001, Richter.

Well Tempered Clavier, Book I.
  3 Columbia D3S-733 (MS-6408, 6538, 6776), Gould (piano).
  2 Columbia M2-32500, Newman (harpsichord).

Béla Bartók

Concerto for Orchestra
  Columbia M-32132, Boulez, N.Y. Phil.
  RCA VICS-1110, Reiner, Chicago Symph.

Ludwig van Beethoven

Diabelli Variations (for piano)
  Philips 9500381, Brendel
  Peters PLE-042, Rosen

Piano Sonata #8, Op. 13 in C min. (Pathetique)
  Columbia MS-6481, Serkin

Piano Sonata #14, Op. 27 #2 in C# min. (Moonlight)
  Philips 6599308, Arrau
  Columbia M-31811, Serkin

String Quartet Op. 131 in C# min.
  Deutsche Grammaphon 2530351, La Salle Quartet

Symphony #3
  Philips 6500986, Haitink, London Philharmonic
  Philips 6500141, Davis, BBC Symph.
  Philips Festivo 6570088, Jochum, Concertgebouw
  London STS-15190, Monteux, Vienna Phil.

Symphony #5
  Deutsche Grammaphon 2530516, Kleiber, Vienna Phil.
  Philips 9500067, Haitink
  Angel S-37463(Q), Jochum, London Symph.
  Philips 802769, Szell, Concertgebouw

Symphony #6
  Philips 6500463, Davis, BBC Symph.
  Odyssey Y-33924, Walter, Columbia Symph.

Symphony #7
  Philips 9500219, Davis, London Symph.
  London STS-15107, Karajan, Vienna Phil.
  RCA LSC-1991, Reiner, Chicago Symph.

Symphony #9
  Seraphim S-60079, Cluytens, Berlin Phil.
  2 Philips 6747390, Haitink, London Phil.
  2 Philips 6700040, Jochum, Concertgebouw
  2 Deutsche Grammaphon 2707109, Karajan, Berlin Phil.

Vincenzo Bellini

Norma
  3 Angel S-3615, Serafin, La Scala
  (Excerpts of above: Angel S-3566)

Alban Berg

Wozzeck
  2 Deutsche Grammaphon 2707023, Böhm

Hector Berlioz

Roméo et Juliette
  Angel S-36038, Giulini, Chicago Symph.

Symphonie fantastique
  Angel S-37138, Martinon

Georges Bizet

Carmen
  3 RCA LSC-6199, Karajan, Vienna Phil.
  (excerpts of above: RCA 2843)

Johannes Brahms

Concerto for Piano #2 in Bb
  RCA VICS-1026, Gilels, Reiner, Chicago Symph.
  Columbia MS-6967, Serkin, Szell, Cleveland Orch.

Symphony #4
  Seraphim S-60101, Giulini
  Philips 6500155, Haitink, Concertgebouw

Tragic Overture
  Philips 6500155, Haitink, Concertgebouw
  Odyssey Y-30851, Walter, Columbia Symph.

Benjamin Britten

Peter Grimes
  3 London 1305, Britten, Royal Opera
  (excerpts of above: London 26004)

Frédéric Chopin

Concerto for Piano #1 in E min.
  Odyssey Y-32369, Gilels, Ormandy, Philadelphia Orch.
  Seraphim S-60066, Pollini, Kletzhi.

24 Preludes
  Deutsche Grammaphon 2530550, Pollini

4 Scherzos
  RCA LSC-2368, Rubinstein

Aaron Copland

Appalachian Spring
    Columbia M-30649, Copland, London Symph.
    Columbia MS-6355, Bernstein, N.Y. Phil.

Claude Debussy

La Mer
    Columbia MS-7361, Boulez

Prélude à l'après-midi d'un faune
    Columbia MS-7361, Boulez
    London STS-15356, Monteux, London Symph.

Josquin des Prez

Motets
    Telefunken Das Alte Werk SAWT 9480-A Ex, Ruhland
    Nonesuch H-71216, Hunter
    BASF KHB 21513, Turner, Pro Cantione Antiqua

Masses
    Nonesuch H-71216, Hunter
    MCA 2507, Greenberg, N.Y. Pro Musica

Gaetano Donizetti

Lucia di Lammermoor
    3 London 13103, Bonynge, Royal Opera
    (excerpts of above: London 26332)

Guillaume Dufay

Chansons
    3 Seraphim S-6092, Munrow, Early Music Consort of London
    Philips 6500085, Beckett, Musica Reservata

Motets
    Deutsche Grammaphon ARC-2533291, Turner, Pro Cantione
    Antiqua

Antonín Dvořák

Symphony #7 in D min.
    London STS-15157, Montex, London Symph.

Symphony #9 (New World)
    Philips 9500511, Davis, Concertgebouw
    Deutsche Grammaphon 138922, Karajan, Berlin Phil.
    2 Columbia MG-30371, Szell, Cleveland Orch.

Edvard Grieg

Peer Gynt Suite
    Deutsche Grammaphon 2530243, Karajan, Berlin Phil.

G. F. Handel

Messiah
    3 Argo D18D-3, Marriner, St. Martin's
    3 Philips SC71AX300, Davis, London Symph.
    (excerpts of above: Philips 6833144)

Water Music
    Deutsche Grammaphon ARC-198365, Wenzinger, Schola
    Oiseau-Lyre 60010, Dart, London Philomusica

F. J. Haydn

String Quartet Op. 76, #3
    Philips 9500157, Quartetto Italiano

Symphony #94 in G (Surprise)
    Philips 9500348, Marriner, Vienna Phil.
    Deutsche Grammaphon 2530628, Jochum, London Phil.

Symphony #101 in D (Clock)
    Deutsche Grammaphon 2530628, Jochum, London Phil.
    RCA AGL1-1275, Reiner

Paul Hindemith

Mathis der Maler Symphony
    Nonesuch 71307, Horenstein, London Symph.
    Columbia MS-6562, Ormandy, Philadelphia Orch.

Gustav Holst

The Planets
    Philips 6500072, Haitink, London Phil.
    Philips 9500425, Marriner, Concertgebouw
    RCA ARL1-1797, Ormandy

Franz Liszt

Hungarian Rhapsodies
  Turnabout 34581, Brendel (piano)

Mephisto-Waltz
  Philips 6500190, Haitink, London Phil.
  Deutsche Grammaphon 2530244, Karajan, Berlin Phil.

Les Preludes
  Philips 839788, Haitink, London Phil.
  Deutsche Grammaphon 139037, Karajan Berlin Phil.

Sonata in Bb min. for piano
  Philips 6500043, Arrau
  RCA LSC-2871, Rubinstein

Guillaume de Machaut

Chansons
  3 Seraphim S-6092, Munrow, Early Music Consort of London
  MCA 2516, New York Pro Music

Gustav Mahler

Das Lied von der Erde
  Philips 6500831, Haitink, Concertgebouw
  Seraphim S-60260, Kletzhi

Symphony #5
  2 Philips 6700048, Haitink, Concertgebouw
  2 Deutsche Grammaphon 2707056, Kubelik, Bavarian Radio
  Symph.

Symphony #9
  2 Odyssey Y2-30308, Walter, Columbia Symph.
  2 Philips 6700021, Haitink, Concertgebouw

Felix Mendelssohn

Concerto for Violin
  Deutsche Grammaphon 2530359, Milstein, Abbado
  RCA LSC-3304, Heifetz, Munch, Boston Symph.
  Columbia MS-6062, Stern, Ormandy

Midsummer Night's Dream Overture
  Columbia MS-7002, Szell
  Philips 9500068, Davis, Boston Symph.

Claudio Monteverdi

Incoronazione di Poppea
    5 Telefunken 635247, Harnoncourt, Con. Mus.
    (excerpts of above: Telefunken 641974)

Vespero della Beata Virgine
    2 Angel S-3837, Munrow, London Early Music Consort
    2 Telefunken 2635045, Harnoncourt, Con. Mus.

Wolfgang Mozart

Don Giovanni
    4 Deutsche Grammaphon 2711006, Böhm
    4 London 1401, Kripps, Vienna Phil.
    excerpts: London 26215, Bonynge, English Chamber Orchestra

The Marriage of Figaro
    4 Philips 6707014, Davis, BBC Symph.
    (excerpts of above: Philips 6500434)
    4 Angel S-3608, Giulini
    (excerpts of above: Angel S-35640)

Serenade in G, K. 555 (Eine Kleine Nachtmusik)
    Oyssey Y-30048, Walter, Columbia Symph.
    Argo ZRG-679, Marriner, St. Martin's Academy

Symphony #40, K. 550 in G min.
    Columbia MS-6494, Walter, Columbia Symph.
    Angel S-36183, Klemperer

Symphony #41 in C (Jupiter)
    London 6479, Giulini
    Deutsche Grammaphon 2530357, Jochum, Boston Symph.
    Columbia MS-6255, Walter, Columbia Symph.

Modest Mussorgsky

Night on Bald Mountain
    London 6785, Solti, London Symphony

Pictures from an Exhibition
    London 6559, Askenazy (piano)
    RCA LSC-2201, Reiner, Chicago Symph.
    Odyssey Y-32223, Szell, Cleveland Orchestra

Johannes Ockeghem

Motets
  Nonesuch H-71336, Blachly

Masses
  Deutsche Grammaphon ARC-2533 145, Turner, Pro Cantione Antiqua
  Deutsche Grammaphon ARC-198 406, Knothe

Carl Orff

Carmina Burana
  Deutsche Grammaphon 139362, Jochum

Johannes Pachelbel

Kanon
  Angel S-37044, Marriner
  Deutsche Grammaphon 2530247, Karajan, Berlin Phil.

Serge Prokofiev

Classical Symphony
  Argo ZRG-719, Marriner
  Deutsche Grammaphon 2530783, Giulini, Chicago Symph.

Romeo and Juliet
  Excerpts: Philips 6500640, DeWaart, Rotterdam Phil.

Giacomo Puccini

Madame Butterfly
  3 Angel S-3604, Santini
  (excerpts from above: Angel S-35821)
  3 London 13110, Karajan, Vienna Phil.
  (excerpts from above: London 26455)

Henry Purcell

Dido and Aneas
  Oiseau-Lyre 60047, Lewis

Maurice Ravel

Boléro
  Philips Festivo 6570092, Monteux, London Symph.
  RCA ARL1-0451, Ormandy
  Philips 9500314, Haitink, Concertgebouw

Ottorini Respighi

Pines of Rome
    RCA ARL1-0415, Ormandy, Philadelphia Orch.

Rimsky-Korsakov

Scheherazade
    London STS-15158, Monteux, London Symph.
    Deutsche Grammaphon 139022, Karajan, Berlin Phil.
    Philips 6500410, Haitink

Arnold Schoenberg

Pierrot Lunaire
    Nonesuch 71251

Franz Schubert

Piano Sonata Op. Posth., D. 960 in Bb
    Columbia M-33932, Serkin

songs
    2 Seraphim S-6083, Baker
    2 Angel S-36341/2, Fischer-Dieskau

String Quintet Op. 114, D 667 in A (Trout)
    Deutsche Grammaphon 2530646, Amadeus Quartet
    Columbia MS-7067, Serkin

Symphony #8 in B min. (Unfinished)
    Deutsche Grammaphon 2530357, Jochum, Boston Symph.
    Columbia MS-6975, Szell, Cleveland

Symphony #9 in C (Great)
    Odyssey Y-34620, Walter
    Deutsche Grammaphon 139043, Karajan, Berlin Phil.
    Philips 9500097, Haitink, Concertgebouw

Die Wintereise
    2 Deutsche Grammaphon 2707028, Fischer-Dieskau

Robert Schumann

Concerto for Piano in A min., Op. 54
    Philips 6500166, Bishop, Davis, BBC Symph.
    Columbia M-31837, Serkin, Ormandy

Dichterliebe
    Deutsche Grammaphon 139109, Fischer-Dieskau

Kreisleriana, Op. 16
   London 6859, Ashkenazy

Jean Sibelius

Finlandia
   Deutsche Grammaphon 139016, Karajan, Berlin Phil.
   Columbia MS-6196, Ormandy, Philadelphia Orch.

Bedřich Smetana

The Moldau (from Ma Vlast)
   Deutsche Grammaphon 139037, Karajan, Berlin Phil.
   Columbia MS-7435, Szell

Richard Strauss

Don Juan
   Deutsche Grammaphon 2530349, Karajan, Berlin Phil.
   Philips 6500481, Haitink

Der Rosenkavaller
   4 Angel S-3563, Karajan
   (excerpts of above: Angel S-35645)

Till Eulenspiegels lustige Streiche
   Deutsche Grammaphon 2530349, Karajan, Berlin Phil.
   Seraphim S-60097, Leinsdorf
   London 6978, Solti, Chicago Symph.

Igor Stravinsky

Le Sacre de printemps (The Rite of Spring)
   Columbia MS-7293, Boulez, Cleveland Orch.
   London 6885, Solti, Chicago Symph.
   Columbia M-31830, Chicago Symph.

Symphony of Psalms
   Columbia MS-6548, Stravinsky

Pitor Tchaikovsky

Concerto for Piano #1 in Bb min.
   London 6360, Ashkenazy, Maazel, London Symph.
   Deutsche Grammaphon 2530677, Berman, Karajan, Berlin Phil.
   RCA VICS-1039, Gilels, Reiner, Chicago Symph.

The Nutcracker
   excerpts: RCA ARL1-0027, Ormandy
   Suite Op. 71A:
   Deutsche Grammaphon 139030, Karajan, Berlin Phil.
   Angel S-36990, Previn, London Symph.

Romeo and Juliet
   Deutsche Grammaphon 2530317, Abbado, Boston Symph.
   London 6209, Karajan, Vienna Phil.

Symphony #6 in B min. (Pathetique)
   Seraphim S-60031, Giulini
   Deutsche Grammaphon 2530774, Karajan

Giuseppe Verdi

La Traviata
   3 RCA LSC-6154, Previtali
   (excerpts from above: RCA LSC 2561)
   2 Deutsche Grammaphon 2707103, Kleiber

Antonio Vivaldi

Seasons
   Argo ZRG-654, Marriner, St. Martin's Academy

Richard Wagner

Die Meistersinger von Nürmberg
   5 Deutsche Grammaphon 2713011, Jochum
   Excerpts: Angel S-36922, Karajan
   Prelude:
   RCA LSC-5007, Reiner, Chicago
   London 7078, Solti, Chicago Symph.
   Columbia MS-6971, Szell, Cleveland Orch.

overtures and preludes
   London 7078, Solti, Chicago Symph.
   Columbia MS-6149, Walter, Columbia Symph.
   Deutsche Grammaphon 136228, Kubelik, Berlin Phil.
   Angel S-37098, Karajan, Berlin Phil.

Tristan und Isolde
   5 Deutsche Grammaphon 2713001, Böhm
   (excerpts of above: Deutsche Grammaphon 136433)
   Prelude:
   Philips 6500932, Haitink, Concertgebouw
   Angel S-37097, Karajan, Berlin Phil.
   Columbia MS-6971, Szell, Cleveland Orch.

Light Classics

This is a short list of some "lighter" classics—works that are considered easily accessible to the newcomer to classical music. They are all orchestral works from the Romantic or Modern Neo-Romantic period, and are generally rather colorful and quite tuneful. Many of these works are staples of "Pops" concerts and outdoor summer evening orchestra concerts.

Adolphe-Charles Adam—Giselle
Samuel Barber—Adagio for Strings
Georges Bizet—L'Arlesienne suite
Ernest Bloch—Schelomo
Alexander Borodin—In the Steppes of Central Asia; Polovetsian Dances
Emmanuel Chabrier—España
Aaron Copland—Rodeo; Appalachian Spring
Léo Delibes—Sylvia; Coppélia
Paul Dukas—Sorcerer's Apprentice
Antonín Dvořák—Slavonic Dances; Carnival Overture
George Enesco—Roumanian Rhapsody #1
Manuel de Falla—Three Cornered Hat; El amor brujo; Nights in the Garden of Spain
Gabriel Fauré—Pavane; Elegy for Cello and Orchestra
George Gershwin—American in Paris; Rhapsody in Blue
Mikhail Ivanovitch Glinka—Ruslan and Ludmila
Edward Grieg—Piano Concerto in A min.; Peer Gynt Suite
Ferde Grofé—Grand Canyon Suite
L. J. F. Herold—overture to Zampa
Franz Liszt—Hungarian Rhapsodies (for piano or orchestra)
Modest Mussorgsky—Night on Bald Mountain
Amilcare Ponchielle—Dance of the Hours
Sergei Prokofiev—Cinderella; Peter and the Wolf; Romeo and Juliet; Classical Symphony
Sergey Rachmaninoff—Piano Concerto #2; Rhapsody on a Theme of Paganini
Maurice Ravel—Bolero; Pavane pour une infante defunte
Ottorino Resphighi—Fountains of Rome; Pines of Rome

Nikolay A. Rimsky-Korsakov—Capriccio espagnol; Scheherezade
Gioacchino Rossini—opera overtures
Camille Saint-Saëns—Carnival of the Animals
Erik Satie—Trois Gymnopédies (for piano or orchestra)
Jean Sibelius—Finlandia
Bedřich Smetana—The Moldau (from Ma Vlast); music from The
   Bartered Bride
Johann Strauss, sr.—Radetzky March, Op. 228
Johann Strauss, Jr.—waltzes
Richard Strauss—Music from Der Rosenkavaller
Pitor Ilyitch Tchaikovsky—The Nutcracker; Romeo and Juliet
   Overture; Capriccio Italien; 1812 Overture; Serenade for String
   Orchestra
Ralph Vaughn Williams—Fantasia on Greensleeves
Carl Maria von Weber—Invitation to the dance

Complete List

The Complete List contains all the composers and works in this guide. The composers are grouped into the chronologically arranged six main stylistic periods (Medieval, Renaissance, Baroque, Classical, Romantic, Modern) and their sub-groups. The main composers of each group are listed (in chronological order) first, in bold type, followed by the lesser composers of that group. A checkmark (√) next to a work means that it is a suggested starting point for that composer. The composers listed on the Core Composers list are signified here by a star (★).

The particular works mentioned on the Complete List are not meant to represent the *only* significant pieces by that composer. Although they often represent what may be called the "heart" of the composer's repertory, they are not the "greatest works", but only samples of them.

Often, categories or genres of works (e.g., piano sonata, madrigal, or symphony) are mentioned but without listing any particular works. This signifies that while the composer contributed significantly to this genre, no especially outstanding or representative works have been singled out for inclusion.

For general comments regarding the inclusion of composers in this guide, see p. 127.

see also
page 88

I.
MEDIEVAL 500-1420

CHANT 500-1100

EARLY POLYPHONY 1000-1300

see also
page 88 **ARS NOVA 1300-1420**—French

★**Guillaume de Machaut** c. 1300-1377

Sacred
—motet
—mass

Secular
√chanson

ARS NOVA—Italian

Francesco Landini c. 1325-1397

Secular

II.
RENAISSANCE 1420-1600

see also
page 89

EARLY 1420-1470—Burgundian

see also
page 89

Gilles Binchois 1400-1460

Secular
—chanson

★**Guillaume Dufay** c. 1400-1474

Sacred
—mass: L'homme armé; Se la face ay pale; Ecce ancilla Domini
—motet: Nuper rosarum flores; O très piteux; Ave Regina caelorum; Alma Redemptoris Mater

Secular
—chanson: Adieu ces bons vins de Lannoys; Resveillés vous; Adieu m'amour, adieu ma joye; Vergine bella

EARLY—English

Leonel Power ?-1445

John Dunstable c. 1370-1453

Sacred

Other composers
Anonymous carols
Music from the Old Hall manuscript

see also
page 90 **MIDDLE 1470-1560**—Burgundian

Antoine Busnois 1430-1492

Secular
—chanson

★**Johannes Ockeghem** 1420-1497

Sacred
—mass: Ecce ancilla Domini; Requiem; Mi-mi
—motet: Intemerata Dei Mater; Alma Redemptoris Mater

Secular
—chanson

Jacob Obrecht 1452-1505

Sacred
—mass: Malheur me bat

Secular
—chanson

★**Heinrich Isaac** c. 1450-1517

Sacred
—music from Choralis Constantius

Secular
—chanson and Lied: Innsbruck ich muss dich lassen; Quis dabit
capiti meo aquam

★**Josquin des Prez** c. 1440/50-1521

Sacred
—mass: √Pange lingua; L'Homme armé
—motet: √ Planxit autem David; √ Miserere mei Deus; Absalon,
fili mi; Illibata Dei Virgo; Alma Redemptoris Mater/Ave Regina;
Ave Maria . . . Virgo serena; Inviolata integra

Secular
—chanson

Other composers

Alexander Agricola 1446-1506
Secular
—chanson

Antoine de Fevin c. 1480-1512

Loyset Compère c. 1450-1518
Secular
—chanson

Pierre de la Rue c. 1460-1518
Sacred
—mass: Requiem
Secular
—chanson

Antoine Brumel c. 1460-1520
Sacred

Jean Mouton c. 1459-1522
Sacred
Secular
—chanson

Pierre Moulu c. 1480/90-c. 1550

Cristobal de Morales c. 1500-1553
Sacred

Nicolas Gombert c. 1500-c. 1556
Sacred
—motet
Secular
—chanson

Jacob Clemens non Papa c. 1510-c. 1556/58
Sacred
—motet
Secular
—chanson

Clément Janequin c. 1485-1560
Secular
—chanson: La Bataille; Le Chant des oiseaux

Jacob Arcadelt c. 1505-c. 1560
Secular
—madrigal

Adrian Willaert c. 1490-1562
Sacred
Secular
—chanson
—madrigal
—instrumental

Claudin de Sermisy c. 1490-1562
Secular
—chanson

Claude Goudimel c. 1505-1572
Sacred
Secular
—chanson

see also
page 90 **MIDDLE**—English

Robert Fayrfax 1464-1521
Sacred

William Cornysh ?-1523
Sacred

King Henry VIII 1491-1547

Christopher Tye c. 1500-1572

see also
page 90 **MIDDLE**—Italian

Antoine Cabezón (Spanish) 1510-1566
organ music

Philippe Verdelot ?-c. 1550
Secular
—madrigal

(Adrian Willaert-see Renaissance, Middle, Burgundian).

see also
page 90 **MIDDLE**—German

Heinrich Finck 1445-1527
Secular
—Lied

Paul Hofhaimer 1459-1537
Secular
—Lied

Ludwig Senfl c. 1486-1542/3
Sacred
Secular
—Lied

(Heinrich Isaac-see Renaissance, Middle, Burgundian).

LATE—1560-1600—Burgundian

see also
page 90

Orlando di Lasso (Roland di Lassus) 1532-1594

Sacred
—motet

Secular
—chanson
—madrigal
—Lied

★ **Pierluigi da Palestrina** c. 1525-1594

Sacred
—mass: Assumpta est Maria; Papae Marcelli; Tu es Petrus
—motet: Super flumina Babylonis
—Stabat Mater

Tomas Luis de Victoria c. 1548-1611

Sacred
—motet: O magnum mysterium

Other Composers

Claude Le Jeune c. 1525/30-1600
Sacred
Secular
—chanson

LATE—Italian

see also
page 90

Cipriano de Rore 1516-1565

Secular
—madrigal

Don Carlo Gesualdo c. 1560-1613

Secular
—madrigal

Other Composers

Andrea Gabrieli c. 1520-1586
Vocal
Instrumental

Giaches de Wert 1535-1596
Sacred
Secular
—madrigal

Luca Marenzio 1553-1599
Secular
—madrigal

Phillipe de Monte 1521-1603
Secular
—madrigal

see also
page 91 **LATE**—English

Thomas Tallis c. 1505-1585

Vocal
—Sacred: Lamentationes Jeremiae

Instrumental
—keyboard

William Byrd 1543-1623

Vocal—Sacred
—mass
—motet
—anthem

Vocal—Secular
—song
—madrigal

Instrumental
—keyboard
—viol music
—consort music

Orlando Gibbons 1583-1625

Vocal—Sacred

Vocal—Secular
—madrigal: The Silver Swan
—consort songs

Instrumental
—keyboard: pavanes
—viol music: pavanes

John Dowland 1562-1626

Vocal—Secular
—lute songs

Other composers

Thomas Morely 1557-1602
Vocal—Secular
Instrumental
—consort music

Thomas Campion 1567-1620
Vocal—Secular
—lute songs

Thomas Weelkes c. 1575-1623
Vocal—Secular
—madrigal

John Bull c. 1562-1628
Instrumental
—harpsichord

John Wilbye 1574-1638
Vocal—Secular
—madrigal

Giles Farnaby c. 1560-1640
Instrumental
—harpsichord

Thomas Tomkins 1572-1656
Vocal—Secular
—madrigal
Instrumental
—keyboard

Thomas Ravenscroft c. 1590-1663
Vocal—Secular

(John Jenkens-see Baroque, Early, English).

III.
BAROQUE 1600-1750

see also
page 91

see also
page 92

EARLY 1600-1700—Italian

Giovanni Gabrieli 1554/7-1612

Vocal
—madrigal
—motet

Instrumental
—ensemble music: brass canzoni

Girolamo Frescobaldi 1583-1643

Instrumental
—keyboard

★ **Claudio Monteverdi** 1567-1643

Vocal
—opera: L'incoronazione di Poppea; L'Orfeo
—madrigal: Il combattimento di Tancredi e Clorinda
√Vespero della Beata Virgine (1610) (Vespers of 1610)

Arcangelo Corelli 1653-1713

Instrumental
—violin sonata
—concerto grosso: Op. 6 (especially #6, "Christmas concerto")

Alessandro Scarlatti 1660-1725

Vocal
—solo cantata
—opera

Other Composers

Giulio Caccini 1546-1618
Vocal
—solo madrigal: Le nuove musiche

Jacopo Peri 1561-1633
Vocal
—opera: Euridice

Luigi Rossi 1597-1653
Vocal
—cantata

Stefano Landi c. 1590-1655
Vocal
—opera: Il Sant' Alessio

Marc' Antonio Cesti 1623-1669
Vocal
—opera

Giacomo Carissimi 1605-1674
Vocal
—cantata
—oratorio

Pier Francesco Cavalli 1602-1676
Vocal
— opera
—cantata

Maurizio Cazzati c. 1620-1677
Instrumental
—trio sonata

Alessandro Stradella 1642-1682
Vocal
—opera
—cantata
—oratorio

Giovanni Legrenzi 1626-1690
Vocal
—opera
—cantata
Instrumental
—ensemble music

Giovanni Battista Vitali c. 1644-1692
Instrumental

Giuseppe Torelli 1658-1709
Instrumental
—concerto: Violin concerti, Op. 8 (12 concerti); trumpet concerti; concerti grossi

Bernardo Pasquini 1637-1710
Vocal
—opera
Instrumental
—keyboard

Giovanni Battista Bassani c. 1657-1716
Vocal
—opera
—oratorio
Instrumental
—sonata

Agostino Steffani 1654-1728
Vocal
—opera
—duet

Antonio Caldara 1670-1736
Vocal
—sacred
—opera
Instrumental
—sonata

see also
page 92 **EARLY**—German

Dietrich Buxtehude c. 1637-1707

Instrumental
—organ

Heinrich Schütz 1585-1672

Vocal
—sacred: Symphoniae Sacrae; Christmas Oratorio; Deutsches Magnificat (1671); Psalms of David; Seven Words from the Cross

Other Composers

Hans Leo Hassler 1564-1612
Vocal
—sacred

Michael Praetorius 1571-1621
Vocal
—sacred

Johann Hermann Schein 1586-1630
Vocal
—sacred

Samuel Scheidt 1587-1654
Vocal
—sacred
Instrumental
—organ

Johann Jakob Froberger 1616-1667
Instrumental
—keyboard

Heinrich Ignaz Franz von Biber 1644-1704
Instrumental

Georg Muffat 1653-1704
Instrumental
—orchestral
—organ

Johann Pachelbel 1653-1706
Vocal
—cantata
Instrumental
—keyboard
—orchestral: Kanon

EARLY—English

see also
page 92

Henry Purcell 1659-1695

Vocal
—opera: √ Dido and Aneas; the Fairy Queen
—ode: √Come ye sons of Art
—sacred: Te Deum and Jubilate in D
—song

Instrumental
—ensemble music
—harpsichord

Other Composers
John Cooperario (Cooper) c. 1575-1626
Instrumental
—ensemble music

Alfonso Ferrabosco (The Younger) c. 1575-1628
Instrumental
—ensemble music
Vocal
—masque

Henry Lawes 1569-1622
Vocal
—masque: Comus

William Lawes 1602-1645
Vocal
—masque
—anthem
Instrumental
—ensemble music

Christopher Simpson c. 1610-1669
Instrumental
—viol

Pelham Humfrey 1647-1674
Vocal
—anthem

Matthew Locke 1630-1677
Vocal
—masque
—anthem
Instrumental
—ensemble music: viol consorts

John Jenkins 1592-1578
Instrumental
—viol fantasias

Jeremiah Clarke c. 1673-1707
Instrumental
—Trumpet Voluntary (for trumpet and orchestra)

John Blow 1648/9-1708
Vocal
—opera: Venus and Adonis
—song
—anthem
—ode: Ode on the Death of Purcell (for two counter-tenors and instrumental accompaniment)

EARLY—French

see also
page 92

Jean-Baptiste Besard 1567-?
Instrumental
—lute

Louis Couperin c. 1626-1661
Instrumental
—harpsichord
—organ

Denis Gaultier c. 1600-1672
Instrumental
—lute

Jacques Champion Chambonnières 1602(?)-1672
Instrumental
—keyboard

Jean-Baptiste Lully 1632-1687
Instrumental
—ballet music
—overtures from operas
Vocal
—opera: Armide; Alceste

Jean-Henri d'Anglebert c. 1628-1691
Instrumental
—keyboard

Marc-Antoine Charpentier 1634-1704
Vocal
—sacred

Michel-Richard de Lalande (Delalande) 1657-1726
Vocal—Sacred
—motet

Marin Marais 1656-1728
Instrumental
—viol
Vocal
—opera

see also
page 93   **LATE**—Italian

★ **Antonio Vivaldi** 1675/8-1741

Vocal
—Gloria in D

Instrumental—orchestral
—concerto: L'estro armonico, Op. 3 (12 concertos for violin and orchestra); √ Seasons (4 concertos for violin and orchestra)

Instrumental—solo
—violin Sonatas

Tomaso Albinoni 1671-1750

Instrumental—orchestral
—concerto: for various instruments
—Adagio (for string orchestra)

Other Composers

Leonardo Vinci 1690-1730
Vocal
—opera

Evaristo Felice dall'Abaco 1675-1742
Instrumental—orchestral
—concerto
Instrumental—sonata

Giovanni Bononcini 1670-1747
Vocal
—opera
Instrumental

Francesco Maria Veracini 1690-c. 1750
Instrumental—solo
—violin sonata

Francesco Feo 1691-1761
Vocal
—opera

Pietro Locatelli 1695-1764
Instrumental—orchestral
—concerto
Instrumental—solo
—violin

(Giovanni Battista Pergolesi-see in Classical, Early, Italian).

LATE—German

see also
page 93

★ Johann Sebastian Bach 1685-1750

Vocal
—cantata: √ #4, Christ lag in Todesbanden; #7, Christ unser
Herr; #21, Ich hatte viel; #31, Der Himmel lacht; #56, Ich will den
Kreuzstab gerne tragen; #61, Nun komm, der Heiden Heiland; #78,
Jesu, der du meine Seele; #80, Ein' feste Burg; #92, Ich hab in
Gottes Herz; #105, Herr, gehe nicht ins Gericht; #106, Gottes Zeit
is die allerbeste Zeit (Actus Tragicus; #161, Komm, du süsse
Todesstunde
—secular cantata: Coffee Cantata; Wedding Cantata
—oratorio: √Passion According to St. Matthew; Passion
According to St. John; Christmas Oratorio (6 cantatas)
—motet
—Mass in B minor
—Magnificat in D

Instrumental—orchestral
√Brandenburg concertos (6); Orchestral Suites

Instrumental—solo
—harpsichord: √ Well Tempered Clavier, Vol. I (24 preludes and
fugues); Inventions; Partitas; Italian Concerto; Goldberg
Variations
—organ
—violin: accompanied and unaccompanied
—undesignated instrumentation: Art of the Fugue; Musical
Offering

★ George Frideric Handel 1685-1759

Vocal
—opera: Giulio Cesare; Serse; Ottone; Alcina
—oratorio: √ Messiah; Acis and Galatea; Alexander's Feast; Ode
for St. Cecilia's Day; Semele; Judas Maccabaeus; Israel in Egypt
—sacred: Te Deum; Chandos Anthems

Instrumental—orchestral
—concerto: 12 Concerti Grossi, Op. 6
 √Water Music
—Royal Fireworks Music

Instrumental—solo
—flute
—harpsichord

Other Composers

Georg Böhm 1661-1733
Instrumental
—organ
—harpsichord

Reinhard Keiser 1674-1739
Vocal
—opera

Johann Joseph Fux 1660-1741
Vocal
—opera
—sacred
Instrumental

Johann Kaspar Ferdinand Fischer c. 1665-1746
Instrumental
—harpsichord
—orchestral

Johann Friedrich Fasch 1668-1758
Vocal
—sacred
Instrumental—orchestral
—overture

see also
page 94   **LATE**—French

François Couperin (Le Grand) 1668-1733

Instrumental
—harpsichord
—chamber music: Concerts royaux

★ **Jean-Philippe Rameau** 1683-1764

Vocal
—opera: Castor et Pollux; Les Indes galantes

Instrumental
—harpsichord

Other Composers

Jean-Baptiste Loeillet 1680-1730
Instrumental
—harpsichord
—flute
—chamber

Jean François Dandrieu 1682-1738
Instrumental
—harpsichord
—organ

André Campra 1660-1744
Vocal
—opera: L'Europe galante

André-Cardinal Destouches 1672-1749
Vocal
—opera

Louis Nicolas Clérambault 1676-1749
Vocal
—cantata
Instrumental

Joseph Bodin de Boismortier 1691-1755
Instrumental
—chamber

François d'Agincourt 1714-1758
Instrumental
—harpsichord

Jacques Hotteterre ?-c. 1760
Instrumental
—flute

Jean Marie Leclair 1697-1764
Instrumental
—orchestral
—chamber
—solo: violin sonata

see also
page 94

IV.
CLASSICAL 1725-1800

see also
page 94

EARLY (ROCOCO) 1725-1775—German

Johann Stamitz 1717-1757

Instrumental
—symphony

Georg Philipp Telemann 1681-1767

Vocal
—sacred
—opera

Instrumental—orchestral
—concerto

Instrumental—solo
—keyboard

Instrumental—chamber

Johann Christian Bach ('London' Bach) 1735-1782

Instrumental—orchestral
—symphony

Instrumental—chamber

Instrumental—solo
—piano

Leopold Mozart 1719-1787

Vocal

Instrumental

Karl Philipp Emanuel Bach 1714-1788

Vocal
—song

Instrumental—orchestral
—concerto

Instrumental—chamber

Instrumental—solo
—clavier (piano, harpsichord or clavichord)

Other composers

Johann Kuhnau 1660-1722
Vocal
—cantata
Instrumental
—keyboard

Georg Matthias Monn 1717-1750
Instrumental—orchestral
—symphony

Karl Heinrich Graun 1704-1759
Vocal
—opera
—sacred
Instrumental—orchestral
—symphony
Instrumental—chamber

Christopher Graupner 1683-1760
Vocal
—cantata
Instrumental—orchestral
—concerto

Johann Schobert 1720-1767
Instrumental—solo
—piano sonata

Gottlieb Muffat 1690-1770
Instrumental—solo
—organ
—harpsichord

Johann Joachim Quantz 1697-1773
Vocal
—song
Instrumental—orchestral
—flute concerto
Instrumental—solo
—flute sonata

Georg Christoph Wagenseil 1715-1777
Instrumental—orchestral
—symphony
Instrumental—solo
—sonata

Christian Cannabich 1731-1798
Instrumental—orchestral
—symphony

Instrumental—chamber

see also
page 95   **EARLY**—English

William Boyce 1710-1779

Instrumental—orchestral
—symphony

Other Composers

William Croft 1678-1727

John Gay (librettist) 1685-1732
Vocal
—opera: The Beggar's Opera

Maurice Greene 1695-1775
Vocal
—anthem
Instrumental—solo
—organ

Thomas Augustine Arne 1710-1788
Vocal
—opera (masque)

EARLY—Italian

see also
page 95

Giovanni Battista Pergolesi 1710-1736

Vocal
—opera: La Serva padrona
—sacred: Stabat Mater

Domenico Scarlatti 1685-1757

Instrumental—solo
—harpsichord

Other Composers

Francesco Antonio Bonporti 1672-1749
Instrumental—solo
—piano sonata

Francesco Geminiani 1687-1762
Instrumental—orchestral
—concertio grosso
Instrumental—solo
—violin sonata

Nicola Antonio Porpora 1686-1768
Vocal
—opera

Giuseppe Tartini 1692-1770
Instrumental—orchestral
—symphony
—concerto
Instrumental—solo
—violin sonata

Niccolò Jommelli 1714-1774
Vocal
—opera

Giovanni Battista Sammartini 1701-1775
Instrumental—orchestral
—symphony
Instrumental—chamber

Jean-Jacques Rousseau (French) 1712-1778
Vocal
—opera: Le Devin du village

Johann Adolph Hasse (German) 1699-1783
Vocal
—opera
—sacred

Padre Antonio Soler (Spanish) 1729-1783
Instrumental—solo
—harpsichord

Baldassare Galuppi 1706-1785
Vocal
—opera
Instrumental—orchestral
—symphony
Instrumental—solo
—harpsichord

see also
page 96 **LATE 1750-1800**—German

★**Wolfgang Amadeus Mozart** 1756-1791

Vocal
—sacred: Mass in C, K. 311 (Coronation); Mass in C min., K. 427 (The Great); √ Requiem, K. 626; Ave, verum corpus, K. 618
—opera: Idomeneo; Die Entführung aus dem Serail (Abduction from the Seraglio); √ Le nozze di Figaro (The Marriage of Figaro); Don Giovanni; Così fan tutte; Die Zauberflöte (The Magic Flute)

Instrumental—orchestral—symphony
—#25, K. 183 in G min.; #29, K. 201 in A; #35, K. 385 in D (Haffner); #36, K. 425 in C (Linz); #38, K. 504 in D (Prague); #39, K. 543 in Eb; √ #40, K. 550 in G min.; #41, K. 551 in C (Jupiter)

Instrumental—orchestral—concerto
—piano: #9, K. 271 in Eb; #15, K. 450 in Bb; #17, K. 453 in G; #19, K. 459 in F; #20, K. 466 in D min.; √ #21, K. 467 in C; #24, K. 491 in C min.; #25, K. 503 in C; #27, K. 595 in Bb
—violin: #3, K. 216 in G; #4, K. 218 in D; #5, K. 219 in A
—violin and viola: K. 364 in Eb (Sinfonia concertante)
—clarinet: K. 622 in A
—flute: #1, K. 313 in G; #2, K. 314 in D
—horn: K. 412; K. 417; K. 447; K. 495

Instrumental—orchestral—divertimento
—#15, K. 287 in Bb (strings and two horns)

Instrumental—orchestral—serenade
—#7, K. 250 in D (Haffner); #10, K. 361 in Bb (13 wind instruments); √ K. 555 in G (Eine Kleine Nachtmusik) (for string orchestra)

Instrumental—orchestral—overtures to operas

Instrumental—chamber
—string quartet: #14-19 (Haydn quartets)
—string quintet: K. 515 in C; K. 516 in G min.
—Quintet in A for Clarinet and Strings, K. 581
—Quintet in Eb for Horn and Strings, K. 407
√Quintet in Eb for Piano and Winds, K. 452
—Trio in Eb for Clarinet, Viola and Piano, K. 498
—sonata for two pianos: K. 448 in D; K. 497 in F

Instrumental—solo—piano
—sonata
—Fantasia and Sonata in C min., K.475 and 457

Instrumental—solo—violin
—sonata

★ **Franz Joseph Haydn** 1732-1809

Vocal
—oratorio: The Creation; The Seasons
—mass: Missa in tempore belli (Paukenmesse, or Mass in Time of War); Lord Nelson Mass (Imperial, or Coronation Mass)

Instrumental—orchestra
—symphony: #6 in D (Le Matin); #7 in C (Le Midi); #8 in G (Le Soir); #26 in D min. (Lamentatione); #31 in D (Hornsignal); #44 in E min. (Trauersymphonie); √ #45 in F# min. (Farewell); #47 in G; #49 in F min. (La Passione); #54 in G; #56 in C; #57 in D; #73 in D (La Chasse); #82-87 (Paris Symphonies—esp. #85 in Bb [La Reine]); #88 in G; #92 in G (Oxford); #93-98 and 99-104 (two sets of London or Salomon symphonies—esp. √ #94 in G (Surprise), #95 in C min., #96 in D (The Miracle), #100 in G (Military), √ #101 in D (Clock), #102 in Bb, #103 in Eb (Drum Roll), 104 in D (London)).
—Trumpet Concerto in Eb

Instrumental—chamber
—string quartet: Op. 17 (6 quartets); Op. 20 (6 quartets—esp. #2, 5, 6); Op. 33 (Russian) (6 quartets—esp. #3); Op. 42 in D min.; Op. 50 (Prussian) (6 quartets); Op. 54 (3 quartets); Op. 55 (3 quartets); Op. 64 (6 quartets); Op. 71 (3 quartets); Op. 74 (3 quartets); Op. 76 (6 quartets—esp. √ #3); Op. 77 (2 quartets—esp. #2)

Instrumental—solo
—piano sonata

★ **Ludwig van Beethoven** 1770-1827

Vocal
—opera: Fidelio
—sacred: Mass in D (Missa Solemnis)

Instrumental—orchestral—symphony
—#1-9, esp. 3, √ 5, √ 6, 9

Instrumental—orchestral—concerto
—piano: #1-5, esp. # 5 in Eb (Emperor)
—violin: Op. 61 in D
Instrumental—orchestral—overture
—Leonore #3: Egmont

Instrumental—chamber
—string quartet: Op. 59 (3 quartets) (Rasumovsky); Op. 74 in Eb (Harp); Op. 95 in F min.; Op. 127 in Eb; Op. 130 in Bb; √ Op. 131 in C# min.; Op. 133 in Bb (Grosse Fugue); Op. 135 in F
—Trio for Violin, Cello and Piano, Op. 97 in Bb (Archduke)
—Trio for Clarinet (or Violin), Cello and Piano, Op. 11 in Bb

Instrumental—solo—piano
—sonata: 32 sonatas—esp.: #5, Op. 10 (#1) in C min.; √ #8, Op. 13 in C min. (Pathetique); #14, Op. 14 (#2) in C# min. (Moonlight); #21, Op. 53 (Waldstein); #23, Op. 57 in F min. (Appassionata); #26, Op. 81a in Eb (Les Adieux); #28, Op. 101 in A; #29, Op. 106 in Bb (Hammer Klavier); #30, Op. 109 in E; #31, Op. 110 in Ab; #32, Op. 111 in C min.
—6 Bagatelles, Op. 126
—Diabelli Variations, Op. 120

Instrumental—solo—violin
—Sonata, Op. 47 (Kreutzer)

Instrumental—solo—cello
—Two Sonatas, Op. 102 (#1 and 2)

Other Composers

Karl Ditters von Dittersdorf 1739-1799
Instrumental
—orchestral
—chamber

Karl Stamitz 1745-1801
Instrumental—orchestral
—symphony

Michael Haydn 1737-1806
Vocal
—sacred
Instrumental

Joseph Wölfl (Woelfl) 1773-1812
Vocal
—opera
Instrumental

Johann Baptist Wanhall 1739-1813
Instrumental
—symphony

Johann Friedrich Reichardt 1752-1814
Vocal
—song

Leopold Anton Koželuch 1752-1818
Instrumental
—piano

Johann Wilhelm Hässler 1747-1822
Instrumental
—piano sonata

Emanuel Aloys Förster 1748-1823
Instrumental

Muzio Clementi 1752-1832
Instrumental
—piano

see also
page 97
LATE—French

Christoph Willibald Gluck 1714-1787

Vocal
—opera: Orfeo ed Euridice; Iphigénie en Aulide; Alceste

Other Composers

Nicolas Dalayrac 1753-1809
Vocal
—opera
Instrumental

Francois Joseph Gossec 1734-1829
Instrumental—orchestral
—symphony

see also
page 97
LATE—Italian

Luigi Boccherini 1743-1805

Instrumental
—chamber

Luigi Cherubini 1760-1842

Vocal
—opera: Médée

Instrumental
—orchestral

Other Composers

Niccolò Piccinni 1728-1800
Vocal
—opera

Gasparo Spontini 1774-1851
Vocal
—opera: La Vestale

V.
ROMANTIC 1800-1900

see also
page 97

CONSERVATIVE

see also
page 98

Carl Maria von Weber 1786-1826

Vocal
—opera: Der Freischutz

Instrumental—orchestral
—opera overtures
—Invitation to the Dance
—Konzertstück, Op. 79 in F min, for orchestra and piano

★ **Franz Schubert** 1797-1828

Vocal
—Lied: over 600 songs, esp. the three main song cycles: Die Schöne
Müllerin; √ Die Winterreise; Schwanengesang

Instrumental—orchestral
—symphony: √ #8 in B min. (The Unfinished); #9 in C
(The Great)
—overture: Rosamunde

Instrumental—chamber
—string quartet: #12, D. 703 in C min. (Quartettstatz); #13, D. 804
in A min.; #14, D. 810 in D min. (Death and the Maiden)
—string quintet: √ Op. 114, D. 667 in A (Trout); Op. 163, D. 956
in C
—piano duet: Grand Duo in C, D. 812; Fantasy in F min., D. 940;
Rondo in A, D. 951
—Octet for Strings and Winds, Op. 166, D. 803 in F

Instrumental—solo—piano
—sonatas—esp. √ Op. Posth., D. 960 in Bb
—6 Moments musicaux, Op. 94, D. 780
—Impromptus, Op. 90, D. 899 and Op. 142, D. 935

★ **Felix Mendelssohn** 1809-1847

Vocal—sacred
—oratorio: St. Paul; Elijah

Instrumental—orchestral—symphony
—#3 (Scottish); √ #4 (Italian); #5 (Reformation)

Instrumental—orchestral—concerto
—piano: #1 in G min.; #2 in D min.
—violin: Violin Concerto in E min.

Instrumental—orchestral—overture
— / Midsummer Night's Dream; Hebrides (Fingal's
Cave); Ruy Blas

Instrumental—chamber
—Octet in Eb for Strings, Op. 20

Instrumental—solo
—piano: Variations sérieuses in D min.; Songs without Words
—organ: 3 Preludes and Fugues, Op. 37; 6 Sonatas, Op. 65
—cello: Sonata #1 for Cello and Piano, Op. 45; Sonata #2 for Cello
and Piano, Op. 58

★ **Frédéric Chopin** 1810-1849

Instrumental—orchestral
—concerto, piano: √ #1, E min.; #2, F min.

Instrumental—solo—piano
—sonata: #2 in Bb min., Op. 35; #3 in B min., Op. 58
√Four Scherzos—esp. #2, Op. 31 in Bb min.
√Four Ballades—esp. # 3, Op. 47 in Ab
√24 Preludes, Op. 28
—Nocturnes—esp. 3 Nocturnes in Bb min., Eb, B, Op. 9; Op. 23
(#1 in C# min.); Op. 37 (#2 in G); Op. 48 (#1 in C min.)
—Waltzes
—Mazurkas—esp. Op. 50 (#3); Op. 56 (#3)
—Polonaises: 2 Polonaises in C# min., Eb min., Op. 26;
2 Polonaises in A, C min., Op. 40; Op. 44 in F# min.; Op. 53 in Ab
—Barcarolle, Op. 60 in F#
—Fantasie-Impromptu in C# min., Op. 66
—Fantasie in F min., Op. 49
—Andante Splanato and Grande Polonaise, Op. 22
—Etudes, Op. 10 and Op. 25

★ **Robert Schumann** 1810-1856

Vocal
—Lied: song cycles: √ Dichterliebe; Liederkreis, Op. 24; Frauen-
liebe und-leben

Instrumental—orchestral
—symphony: 1-4
—concerto, piano: √ Piano Concerto, Op. 54 in A min.
—concerto, cello: Cello Concerto, Op. 129 in A min.
—Manfred Overture

Instrumental—chamber
—Piano Quintet for Strings and Piano, Op. 44 in Eb

Instrumental—solo
—piano: √ Fantasy in C, Op. 17;   √ Kreislerliana, Op. 16 (8
fantasies); Carnaval (20 pieces); Davidsbündlertanze (18 pieces);
Album for the Young; Fantasiestücke; Symphonic études, Op. 13;
Papillons, Op. 2

★**Johannes Brahms** 1833-1897

Vocal
—Ein deutsches Requiem (for Bass solo, chorus, orchestra)
—Alto Rhapsody (for alto solo, male chorus, orchestra)
—Shicksaslied (for chorus and orchestra)
—Lied—esp. Four Serious Songs, Op. 121

Instrumental—orchestral
—symphony: 1-4
—concerto, piano: #1 in D min.;   √ #2 in Bb
—concerto, violin: Violin Concerto in D
—concerto, Double Concerto for Violin and Cello in A min.
√Tragic Overture
—Academic Festival Overture
—Variations on a Theme by Haydn in Bb

Instrumental—chamber
—Sextet for Strings, Op. 36 in Bb
—Quartet for Piano and Strings, Op. 25 in G min.
—Quartet for Piano and Strings, Op. 60 in C min.
—Quintet for Piano and Strings, Op. 34 in F min. (1864 version)
—Quintet for Strings, Op. 88 in F
—Quintet for Strings Op. 111 in G
√Quintet for Clarinet and Strings, Op. 115 in B min.
—Trio for Piano, Violin and Viola, Op. 87 in C
—Trio for Piano, Violin and Viola, Op. 101 in C min.-
—Trio for Piano, Violin and Horn (or Cello or Viola), Op. 40 in
Eb

Instrumental—solo
—piano: Sonata, Op. 5 in F min.; 8 Pieces, Op. 76; 2 Rhapsodies, Op. 79; 7 Pieces, Op. 116; 3 Intermezzi, Op. 117; / 6 Pieces, Op. 118; 4 Pieces, Op. 119
—violin sonatas
—cello sonatas
—clarinet sonatas
—organ: Chorale Preludes

Other Composers

Johann Ladislaus Dussek 1760-1812
Instrumental
—piano: sonatas

Friedrich Kuhlau 1786-1832
Instrumental
—piano
—flute

Johann Nepomuk Hummel 1778-1837
Instrumental—orchestral
—Trumpet Concerto in Eb
Instrumental—chamber
—septets for piano, strings, winds—esp. Op. 74
—Quintet, Op. 87
Instrumental—solo
—piano—esp. Sonata, Op. 81 in F# min.

John Field 1782-1837
Instrumental—solo
—piano: nocturnes

Johann Baptist Cramer 1771-1858
Instrumental—solo
—piano—etudes

Ludwig Spohr 1784-1859
Vocal
—opera: Jessonda
Instrumental—orchestral
—symphony: Die Weihe der Töne, Op. 80
—concerto
Instrumental—chamber
—double string quartets
—Nonet, Op. 31

Karl Loewe 1796-1869
Vocal
—Lied

Ignaz Moscheles 1794-1870
Instrumental—solo
—piano

Joseph Joachim Raff 1822-1882
Instrumental

Robert Volkmann 1815-1883
Instrumental
—chamber

Robert Franz 1815-1892
Vocal
—Lied

Carl Reinecke 1824-1910
Instrumental—orchestral
—concerto

GRANDIOSE

see also
page 99

★ **Hector Berlioz** 1803-1869

Vocal
—opera: Les Troyens
—Damnation of Faust (for solo voices, chorus, orchestra)
√Roméo et Juliette (for solo voices, chorus, orchestra)
—Te Deum (for tenor, 3 choirs, orchestra, brass bands)
— Requiem (for tenor, chorus, orchestra, brass bands)
—L'Enfance du Christ (for solo voices, chorus, orchestra)

Instrumental—orchestral
/Symphone fantastique
—Harold in Italy (orchestra with solo viola)

★ **Richard Wagner** 1813-1883

Vocal
—opera: Der fliegende Holländer (The Flying Dutchman);
Tannhäuser; Lohengrin; Das Ring des Nibelungen (cycle of 4
operas: Das Rheingold, Die Walküre, Siegfried, Gotterdam-
merung); / Tristan und Isolde; / Die Meistersinger von
Nürnberg; Parsifal

Instrumental—orchestral
—opera overtures and excerpts

Instrumental—chamber
—Siegfried Idyll (also in orchestral version)

★ **Franz Liszt** 1811-1886

Instrumental—orchestral
/Les Preludes
—Orpheus
—Hamlet
/Faust Symphony
—Dante Symphony
/Mephisto-Waltz
—Totentanz (for piano and orchestra)
—Hungarian Fantasia (for piano and orchestra)
—concerto, piano: / #1 in Eb; #2 in A min.

Instrumental—solo
—piano: / Sonata in B min.; 24 Grandes Études; Études
d'exécution transcendante—esp. #4 (Mazeppa); Etudes d'exécution
transcendante d'après Paganini—esp. #3 (La campanella); 3 Études
de Concert; Harmonies poétiques et religieuses; Années de
pèlerinage; Consolations; Hungarian Rhapsodies (19)—
 / esp. #2 and 15 (also in orchestral version)
—organ

★ **Anton Bruckner** 1824-1896

Vocal
—Mass in D min.
—Te Deum

Instrumental—orchestral
—symphony: / #4 in Eb (Romantic); #7 in E; #8 in C min.;
#9 in D min.

★ **Gustav Mahler** 1860-1911

Vocal
—song cycle (for solo voice with orchestra): / Das Lied von der
Erde; Des Knaben Wunderhorn; Kindertotenlieder; Songs of a
Wayfarer

Instrumental—orchestral
—symphony: 1-9—esp. / #5, / 9

★**Richard Strauss** 1864-1949

Vocal
—opera: √ Elektra; Der Rosenkavaller
—song

Instrumental—orchestral
—Tod und Verklärung (Death and Transfiguration)
—Also sprach Zarathustra
 √Till Eulenspiegels lustige Streiche
—Don Quixote
—Don Juan
—Ein Heldenleben (A Hero's Life)
—Sinfonia domestica

Other Composers

Niccolò Paganini 1782-1840
Instrumental—orchestral
—Violin Concerto #1 in D
Instrumental—solo
—violin: caprices

Sigismond Thalberg 1812-1871
Instrumental
—piano

Peter Cornelius 1824-1874
Vocal
—opera: Der Barbier von Bagdad
—Lied

Charles-Henri Valentin Alkan 1813-1888
Instrumental
—piano

IMPRESSIONISM   see also
page 100

★**Claude Debussy** 1862-1918

Vocal
—opera: Pelléas et Mélisande
—song

Instrumental—orchestral
√Prélude à l'après-midi d'un faune
√La Mer
—Noctures
—Images
—Danse sacrée et danse profane

Instrumental—chamber
—String Quartet #1
—Sonata for Harp, Flute and Viola

Instrumental—solo
—piano: Rêverie; Clair de lune (from Suite bergamasque);
Estampes; Images (book I); Children's Corner; √ 12 Preludes
(book I)

Maurice Ravel

Instrumental—orchestral
√Pavane pour une infante défunte (Pavane for a dead princess
(also for piano)
—Daphnis et Cloé
—Rapsodie espagnole
√Bolero
√Ma Mère l'Oye (Mother Goose Suite) (also for piano duet)
—La Valse
—Alborada del gracioso
—Piano concerto in G
—Piano concerto in D (for the left hand)

Instrumental—chamber
—String quartet
—Introduction and Allegro for Harp, String Quartet, Flute and
Clarinet
—Trio for Piano, Violin and Cello

Instrumental—solo
—piano: Gaspard de la nuit; Valses nobles et sentimentales; Le
Tombeau de Couperin; Jeaux d'eau; √ Miroirs

Other Composers

Charles Griffes 1884-1920
Instrumental
—orchestral
—chamber

Erik Satie 1866-1925
Instrumental—solo
—piano: Trois Gymnopédies

ROMANTIC—Italian

see also
page 100

Vincenzo Bellini 1801-1835

Vocal
—opera: I Puritani; La Sonnambula; √ Norma

★ **Gaetano Donizetti** 1797-1848

Vocal
—opera: Lucrezia Borgia; √ Lucia di Lammermoor; √ La Fille du
regiment; L'elisir d'amore; Don Pasquale; Maria Stuarda

Giacomo Meyerbeer

Vocal
—opera: Robert le Diable; Les Huguenots; Le Prophète;
L'Africaine

Gioacchino Rossini 1792-1868

Vocal
—opera: √ Il barbiere di Siviglia (The Barber of Seville); Le
Comte Ory
—sacred: Stabat Mater

Instrumental—orchestral
—opera overtures

★ **Giuseppe Verdi** 1813-1901

Vocal
—opera: Macbeth; Rigoletto; Il Trovatore (The Troubador);
 √ La Traviata (The Lost One); Un ballo in maschera (The Masked
Ball); Aïda; √ Otello; Falstaff; Rigoletto; La Forza del destino
(The Force of Destiny); Don Carlo
—sacred: Requiem

Ruggiero Leoncavallo 1858-1919

Vocal
—opera: I Pagliacci

★ **Giacomo Puccini** 1858-1924

Vocal
—opera: La Bohème; Tosca; √ Madame Butterfly; Turandot;
Manon Lescaut

Pietro Mascagni 1863-1945

Vocal
—opera: Cavalleria rusticana

see also
page 100

ROMANTIC—French—Early

André Ernest Modeste Grétry 1741-1813
Vocal
—opera

L. J. F. Herold 1791-1833
Vocal
—opera: Le Pré aux clercs; Zampa
Instrumental—orchestral
—overture to Zampa

François-Adrien Boiedlieu 1775-1834
Vocal
—opera: La Dame Blanche

Jean François le Sueur 1760-1837
Vocal
—opera
—sacred

Adolphe-Charles Adam 1803-1856
Vocal
—opera
Instrumental—orchestral
—ballet music: Giselle

Jacques Fromenthal Halévy 1799-1862
Vocal
—opera: La Juive

D. F. E. Auber 1782-1871
Vocal
—opera: La Muette de Patrici

Felicien David 1810-1876
Vocal
—opera
Instrumental
—orchestral

Ambroise Thomas 1811-1896
Vocal
—opera: Mignon

ROMANTIC—French—Late

Georges Bizet 1838-1875

Vocal
—opera: Carmen

Instrumental—orchestral
—L'Arlésienne suite
—Symphony #1 in C

César Franck 1822-1893

Instrumental—orchestral
—Symphony in D min.
—Symphonic Variations (for piano and orchestra)

Instrumental—chamber
—String Quartet in D
—Piano Quintet in F min. (for piano and strings)

Instrumental—solo
—piano: Prelude, Chorale and Fugue; Prelude, Aria and Finale
—organ

Charles François Gounod 1818-1893

Vocal
—opera: Faust; Roméo et Juliette
—sacred: La Redemption; Missa Solennelle

Camille Saint-Saëns 1835-1921

Vocal
—opera: Samson et Dalila

Instrumental—orchestral
√Symphony #3 in C min. (Organ Symphony)
—Cello Concerto #1 in A min.
—Piano Concerto #4 in C min.
—Violin Concerto #3 in B min.
√Carnival of the Animals
—Danse macabre

Instrumental—chamber
—Septet for Strings, Piano and Trumpet

Gabriel Fauré 1845-1924

Vocal
√Requiem (for chorus and orchestra)
√chanson: La Bonne Chanson, Op. 61 (song cycle)

Instrumental—orchestral
—Pavane
—Dolly (also for piano duet)
—Pelléas et Mélisande
—Ballade (for piano and orchestra)
—Elegy for Cello and Orchestra (or piano)

Instrumental—chamber
—Piano Quintet #1, Op. 15 in C min.
√Piano Quintet #2, Op. 45 in G min.
√Trio for Violin, Cello, Piano in D min., Op. 120
—string Quartet in E min.
—Violin Sonata

Other Composers

Léo Delibes 1836-1891
Vocal
—opera: Lakmé
Instrumental—orchestral
—ballet music: Sylvia; Coppelia

Édouard Lalo 1823-1892
Instrumental—orchestral
—Symphony in G min.
—Cello Concerto
—Symphonie espagnole (for violin and orchestra)

Ernest Chausson 1855-1899
Instrumental—orchestral
—Poème for Violin and Orchestra, Op. 25
Instrumental—chamber
—Piano Quartet (for piano and strings)
—String Quartet in A

Jules Massenet 1842-1912
Vocal
—opera: Manon
Instrumental—orchestral
—Le Cid

Vincent d'Indy 1851-1931
Vocal
—opera: Fervaal
Instrumental
—orchestral: Jour d'été à la montagne (Symphony on a French
Mountain Air) (for orchestra and piano); Istar
—solo: Violin Sonata

Paul Dukas 1865-1935
Instrumental
—orchestral: Sorcerer's Apprentice

Albert Roussel 1869-1937
Vocal
—orchestral
—chamber

Gustave Charpentier 1860-1956
Vocal
—opera: Louise

ROMANTIC—Russian see also
page 100

Modest Mussorgsky 1839-1881

Vocal
—opera: Boris Godunov
—song: song cycles—Songs and Dances of Death; The Nursery

Instrumental—orchestral
√Night on Bald Mountain
√Pictures from an Exhibition (arranged by Ravel-also in a piano
version)
—music from opera Khovanschina

Alexander Borodin 1833-1887

Instrumental—orchestral
—In the Steppes of Central Asia
 √Polovetsian Dances (from opera Prince Igor)
—symphonies
—Nocturne for String Orchestra (from String Quartet #2)

★ Pitor Ilyitch Tchaikovsky 1840-1893

Vocal
—opera: Eugene Onegin

Instrumental—orchestral
—symphony: #4 in F min.; #5 in E min.; √ #6 in B min.
(Pathetique)
—ballet music: Swan Lake; The Sleeping Beauty; √ The
Nutcracker
—concerto, piano: √ Piano Concerto #1 in Bb min.
—concerto, violin: Violin Concerto in D
 √Romeo and Juliet Overture
—Capriccio Italien
—Francesca da Rimini
—Marche Slave
—1812 Overture
—Serenade for String Orchestra

Nikolay A. Rimsky-Korsakov 1844-1908

Vocal
—opera: Le Coq d'Or (The Golden Cockerel)

Instrumental—orchestral
—Capriccio espagnol
—Scheherezade
—Russian Easter

Sergey Rachmaninoff 1873-1943

Instrumental—orchestral
—The Isle of the Dead
—Rhapsody on a Theme of Paganini
—concerto, piano: #2, 3

Instrumental—solo
—piano: Preludes, Op. 23

Other Composers

Mikhail Ivanovitch Glinka 1804-1857
Vocal
—opera: A Life for the Tsar; Ruslan and Ludmila *overture*

Alexander Sergeyervitch Dargomyzsky 1813-1869
Vocal
—opera: Russalka; The Stone Guest

Anton Grigorievitch Rubinstein 1829-1894
Instrumental
—orchestral: Piano Concerto in D min.

Mily Alexeyevitch Balakirev 1837-1910
Instrumental—orchestral
—Russia
Instrumental—solo
—piano: The Lark

Alexander Glazunov 1865-1936
Instrumental
—orchestral: Raymonda

ROMANTIC—Miscellaneous

see also
page 101

Jacques Offenbach (French) 1819-1880

Vocal
—opera: Les Contes d'Hoffman (The Tales of Hoffman); Orphée aux enfers (Orpheus in the Underworld); La Vie parisienne

Instrumental
—orchestral: Gaité Parisienne (arranged by Rosenthal)

Bedřich Smetana (Bohemian) 1824-1884

Vocal
—opera: Bartered Bride

Instrumental—orchestral
—Má Vlast (6 pieces including The Moldau)
—music from opera The Bartered Bride

Johann Strauss (Jr.) (The Younger) (Austrian) 1825-1899

Vocal
—opera: Die Fledermaus; The Gypsy Baron

Instrumental—orchestral
—waltzes: Le Beau Danube

Hugo Wolf (Austrian) 1860-1903

Vocal
—Lied

Antonín Dvořák (Czech) 1841-1903

Vocal
—opera: Rusalka

Instrumental—orchestral
—symphony: √ #7 in D min.; #8 in G; #9 in E min. (New World)
—Slavonic Dances
—Carnival Overture
—Cello Concerto in g min.

Instrumental—chamber
—string quartet: √ #6 in F, Op. 96 (American); #7 in Ab, Op. 105;
#13 in G, Op. 106
—String Quintet in Eb, Op. 97
—Quintet for Piano and Strings in A, Op. 81

Eduard Grieg (Norwegian) 1843-1907

Instrumental—orchestral
—Peer Gynt Suite
—Piano Concerto in A min.

Instrumental—solo
—piano
—violin sonatas
—cello sonata

Instrumental—chamber

Edward Elgar (English) 1857-1934

Vocal
—The Dream of Gerontius (for solo voices, chorus, orchestra)

Instrumental—orchestral
√Enigma Variations
—Cockaigne Overture
—Falstaff
—Pomp and Circumstance marches
—Introduction and Allegro for Strings, Op. 47
—Serenade in E min. for Strings, Op. 20

Gustav Holst (English) 1874-1934

Instrumental—orchestral
—The Planets

Ottorino Respighi (Italian) 1879-1936

Instrumental—orchestral
—Fountains of Rome
 √Pines of Rome
—Ancient Airs and Dances
—Feste Romane
—Gli Uccell (The Birds)

Other Composers

Johann Strauss (Sr.) (Austrian) 1804-1849
Instrumental
—orchestral: Radetzhy March, Op. 288

Louis Moreau Gottschalk (American) 1829-1869
Instrumental—solo
—piano

Amilcare Ponchielle (Italian) 1834-1886
Instrumental
—orchestral: Dance of the Hours (from opera La Gioconda)

Emmanuel Chabrier (French) 1841-1894
Instrumental
—orchestral: España

Franz von Suppé (Belgian) 1819-1895
Instrumental—orchestral
—overture

William S. Gilbert 1836-1911 and Sir Arthur Sullivan 1842-1900
(English)
Vocal
—operetta: H.M.S. Pinafore; Pirates of Penzance

Edward Alexander MacDowell (American)
Instrumental—orchestral
—Piano Concerto #2
Instrumental—solo
—piano: Keltic Piano Sonata

Isaac Albéniz (Spanish) 1860-1909
Instrumental
—orchestral: Iberia (also for piano)
—solo: piano

Alexander Scriabin (Russian) 1872-1915
Instrumental—orchestral
—Symphony #4 (Poem of Ecstasy); Symphony #5 (Prometheus)
Instrumental—solo
—piano: Sonata #7 in F# (White Mass); Sonata #9 in F (Black Mass)

Max Bruch (German) 1838-1920
Instrumental—orchestral
—Violin Concerto #1 in G min.

Englebert Humperdinck (German) 1854-1921
Vocal
—opera: Hansel und Gretel

Carl Nielsen (Danish) 1865-1931
Instrumental
—orchestral: Symphony #5

Richard Addinsell (English) 1904-1933
Instrumental
—orchestral: Warsaw Concerto (for piano and orchestra)

Frederick Delius (English) 1862-1934
Instrumental—orchestral
—Appalachia
—On Hearing the First Cuckoo in Spring

Joseph Suk (Czech) 1874-1935
Instrumental—orchestral
—string serenades

Arnold Bax (English) 1883-1953
Instrumental
—orchestral
—chamber

VI.
MODERN 1900-Present

see also
page 101

NEO-CLASSICAL

see also
page 102

★ **Béla Bartók** 1881-1945

Instrumental—orchestral
√Concerto for Orchestra
√Music for Strings, Percussion and Celesta
—Violin Concerto (1938)
—Piano Concertos 1-3
—The Miraculous Mandarin

Instrumental—chamber
—String Quartets 1-6
—Sonata for Two Pianos and Percussion

Instrumental—solo
—piano

★ **Paul Hindemith** 1895-1963

Vocal
—opera: Mathis der Maler (Matthias the Painter); Cardillac
—madrigal
—song cycle: Das Marienleben (The Life of Mary)

Instrumental—orchestral
√Symphonic Metamorphoses on a Theme of Weber
√Mathis der Maler Symphony (from the opera)
—Symphony in Bb for Band

Instrumental—chamber

Instrumental—solo
—sonatas for various instruments
—piano: Ludus Tonalis

Francis Poulenc 1899-1963

Vocal
—opera: Les Mamelles de Tiresias (The Beasts of Tiresias)
—Stabat Mater (for chorus, soprano and orchestra)
√Gloria in G (for soprano, chorus and orchestra)

Instrumental—orchestral
—Concert Champêtre (Pastoral Concerto) for Harpsichord or Piano and Small Orchestra

Instrumental—chamber .

★ **Igor Stravinsky** 1882-1971

Vocal
—opera: Oedipus Rex; The Rake's Progress
—Les Noces (The Wedding) (for chorus and orchestra)

Instrumental—orchestral
—The Fire Bird
—Petrouchka
√Le Sacre de printemps (The Rite of Spring)
—Pulcinella Suite
√Dumbarton Oaks Concerto
—Symphony in Three Movements
√Symphony in C
—Ebony Concerto (for clarinet and orchestra)

Instrumental—chamber
—Octet for Winds
—L'Histoire du Soldat (The Soldier's Tale) (for narrator and chamber ensemble)
—Symphonies of Wind Instruments

Dmitri Shostakovich 1906-1975

Vocal
—opera: Lady Macbeth

Instrumental—orchestral
—Symphony #5

Instrumental—chamber
—Piano Quintet, Op. 57

Benjamin Britten 1913-1977

Vocal
—opera: √ Peter Grimes; Rape of Lucretia; Billy Budd; The Turn of the Screw; A Midsummer Night's Dream; Death in Venice
√A Ceremony of Carols (for chorus)
—Rejoice the Lamb (for chorus)
—Curlew River (for chorus)
—War Requiem (for chorus)

Instrumental—orchestral
—The Young Person's Guide to the Orchestra
—Spring Symphony (for orchestra and chorus)

Aaron Copland 1900-

Instrumental—orchestra
—Billy the Kid
✓Rodeo
—Fanfare for the Common Man
✓Appalachian Spring
—Quiet City (for trumpet, English horn and orchestra)
—El Salón Mexico

Olivier Messiaen 1908-

Instrumental—orchestral
✓Turangalîla Symphony
—Chronochromie
—L'Ascension

Instrumental—chamber
✓Quartour pour la fin du temps (Quartet for the End of Time)
(for violin, clarinet, piano, cello)

Instrumental—solo
—piano: Vingt Regards sur l'Enfant Jésus
—organ

Other Composers

Leŏs Janáček 1854-1928
Vocal
—opera: Jenufa
Instrumental
—orchestral: Sinfonietta

Arthur Honegger 1892-1955
Vocal
—oratorio: King David; Jeanne d'Arc au bûcher
Instrumental
—orchestral: Pacific 231

Bohuslav Martinu 1890-1959
Instrumental
—orchestral: Concerto for Double String Orchestra

Zoltan Kodály 1882-1967
Vocal
—opera: Háry János; Szekelyfonó
—Psalmus hungaricus (for chorus and orchestra)
Instrumental
—orchestral
—chamber

Darius Milhaud 1892-1974
Vocal
—opera: Christophe Colombo
Instrumental—orchestral
—Le Boeuf sur le Toit (The Ox on the Roof)
—La Création du monde

Walter Piston 1894-1976
Instrumental—orchestral
—symphonies
—The Incredible Flutist
Instrumental—chamber
—String quartet #5

Michael Tippett 1905-
Vocal
—opera: A Mid Summer Marriage
—oratorio: A Child of Our Time
Instrumental—orchestral
—Concerto for Double String Orchestra
—Concerto for Orchestra

Elliott Carter 1908-
Instrumental—orchestral
—Double Concerto
—Variations for Orchestra
—Concerto for Orchestra
Instrumental—chamber
√Sonata for flute, oboe, cello, harpsichord

Samuel Barber 1910-
Vocal
Instrumental—orchestral
—Knoxville, summer of 1915 (for soprano and orchestra)
—Capricorn Concerto (for flute, oboe, trumpet and orchestra)
—Adagio for Strings (from String Quartet, Op. 11)

Ned Rorem 1923-
Vocal
—song
Instrumental
—orchestral

Daniel Pinkham 1923-
Instrumental
—orchestral
—chamber

NEO-ROMANTIC

see also
page 104

Sergei Prokofiev 1891-1953

Instrumental—orchestral
√Classical Symphony
—Symphony #5 in Bb
√Romeo and Juliet Ballet
—Scythian Ballet
—Lieutenant Kijé Suite
—Peter and the Wolf
—Alexander Nevsky
—Cinderella
√Piano Concerto #3
—Violin Concerto #1 in D
—Violin Concerto #2 in G min.

Instrumental—chamber

Vocal
—opera: Love of Three Oranges

Jean Sibelius 1865-1957

Instrumental—orchestral
—Symphonies #1, 2, 5
√Finlandia
—Valse Triste (from Koulema suite, Op. 44)
—Concerto for Violin in D min., Op. 47

Ralph Vaughn Williams 1872-1958

Instrumental—orchestral
—Fantasia on Greensleeves
—Fantasia on a Theme of Thomas Tallis for Double String
Orchestra and String Quartet
—symphonies
—Lark Ascending for Violin and Orchestra

Other Composers

Victor Herbert 1859-1924
Vocal
—operetta

Ferruccio Busoni 1866-1924
Instrumental

George Gershwin 1898-1937
Instrumental—orchestral
—American in Paris
—Rhapsody in Blue
—Piano Concerto in F
—I Got Rhythm—Variations for Piano and Orchestra
Vocal
—opera: Porgy and Bess
—songs

Manuel de Falla 1876-1946
Instrumental—orchestral
—The Three Cornered Hat Ballet
—El amor brujo
—Nights in the Garden of Spain

Kurt Weill 1900-1950
Vocal
—opera: Three Penny Opera; Mahagonny; Knickerbocker Holiday

George Enesco 1881-1955
Instrumental
—orchestral: Roumanian Rhapsody #1, Op. 11
Instrumental—chamber

Erich Wolfgang Korngold 1897-1957
Instrumental
—orchestral
—chamber

Ernest Bloch 1880-1959
Instrumental—orchestral
—Schelomo—Rhapsody for Cello and Orchestra
Instrumental—chamber
—Quintet for Piano and Strings

Heitor Villa-Lobos 1887-1959
Vocal

Jacqués Ibert 1890-1962
Instrumental
—orchestral: Escales (Port of Call)
Instrumental—chamber

Ferde Grofé 1892-1972
Instrumental
—orchestral: Grand Canyon Suite

Arthur Bliss 1891-1975
Instrumental
—orchestral

William Walton 1902-1977
Vocal
—oratorio: Belshazzar's Feast
—opera: Troilus and Cressida
Instrumental
—orchestral: Viola Concerto
—chamber: Façade (for chamber ensemble with narrator)

Carl Orff 1896-
Vocal
—opera: Der Mond (The Moon)
—Carmina Burana (for orchestra and chorus)

Howard Hanson 1896-
Instrumental
—orchestral

Roy Harris 1898-
Vocal
Instrumental
—orchestral

Aram Khachaturian 1903-
Instrumental
—orchestral: Concerto for Violin and Orchestra

Dmitri Kabalevsky 1904-
Vocal
Instrumental
—orchestral
—solo, piano

Morton Gould 1913-
Instrumental
—orchestral

Alberto Ginastera 1916-
Instrumental
—orchestral

Leonard Bernstein 1918-
Vocal
—Mass
—opera: Trouble in Tahiti
—West Side Story
Instrumental—orchestral
—Fancy Free
—On the Town
—On the Waterfront Suite
—Overture to Candide

ATONALITY
see also
page 104

★ Alban Berg 1885-1935

Vocal
—opera: Wozzeck; Lulu
—Altenberg Lieder. Op. 4 (for voice and orchestra)

Instrumental
—orchestral: Violin Concerto
—chamber: Lyric Suite (for string quartet)

Anton Webern 1883-1945

Vocal

Instrumental—orchestral
—Five Pieces for Orchestra, Op. 10
—Variations for Orchestra, Op. 30

Instrumental—chamber
—Six Bagatelles for String Quartet, Op. 9
—String Quartet, Op. 5
—String Quartet, Op. 28

Instrumental—solo
—piano: Variations, Op. 27

★ **Arnold Schoenberg** 1874-1951

Vocal
—opera: Moses und Aaron
—song cycle: Gurrelieder (for voices and orchestra); Das Buch der hängenden Gärten (Book of the Hanging Gardens) (for voice and piano); Erwartung (for soprano and orchestra; √ Pierrot Lunaire (for voice and chamber ensemble)

Instrumental—orchestral
√Verklärte Nacht (Transfigured Night)
√Five Orchestral Pieces, Op. 16
—Chamber Symphony #1, Op. 9
—Variations for Orchestra, Op. 31

Instrumental—chamber
—string quartet
—String Trio, Op. 45

Instrumental—solo—piano
√Three Pieces, Op. 11
—Six Little Pieces, Op. 19
—Two Pieces, Op. 33a and 33b

Other Composers

Luigi Dallapiccola 1904-1975
Vocal
—Canti di prigionia (for chorus and instruments)
—Cinque canti (for baritone and 8 instruments)
—Sex carmina Alcaei (for soprano and instruments)
—opera: Ulisse

Roger Sessions 1896-
Vocal
—opera: Montezuma
Instrumental—orchestral
—Symphony #3
—Violin Concerto
Instrumental—chamber
—Concertino for Chamber Orchestra
Instrumental—solo
—piano: Sonata #2

Ernest Krenek 1900-
Vocal
—opera: Jonny spielt auf
Instrumental

Milton Babbit 1916-
Instrumental

Pierre Boulez 1925-
Vocal
—Le Marteau sans maître (for alto voice and six instruments)
—Pli selon sli—Portrait of Mallarmé (for soprano and orchestra)
Instrumental
—chamber: Structures I (for two pianos)

see also
page 105 **EXPERIMENTAL**

Charles Ives 1874-1954

Vocal
—songs

Instrumental—orchestral
—The Unanswered Question
√Three Places in New England
—Symphonies 2, 3, 4
√New England Holiday: Washington's Birthday, Decoration Day,
4th of July, Thanksgiving
—Central Park in the Dark
—America Variations

Instrumental—solo
—piano: Concord Sonata

Edgard Varèse 1883-1965

Instrumental
—chamber
—mixed
—electronic
—Intégrales (for woodwinds, brass and percussion)
—Ionisation (13 percussion instruments)

Other Composers
Harry Partch 1901-1974
Instrumental

Otto Luening 1900-
Instrumental
—orchestral
—chamber
—electronic

John Cage 1912-
Mixed Medium

George Rochbert 1918-
Instrumental
—chamber
—solo, piano: 12 Bagatelles

Lukas Foss 1922-
Instrumental
—Baroque Variations

Iannis Xenakis 1922-
Instrumental
—electronic

Gyorgy Ligeti 1923-
Instrumental
—chamber
—electronic

Luigi Nono 1924-
Vocal
—opera
—vocal music with instruments

Luciano Berio 1925-
Vocal
—Circles (for soprano, harp, percussion)
Instrumental
—orchestral: Sinfonia (for orchestra and voices)
—chamber
—electronic: Omaggio a Joyce

Gunther Schuller 1925-
Instrumental
—orchestral: Studies on a Theme of Paul Klee
—chamber: Quartet for Double Basses

Hans Werner Henze 1926-
Vocal
—opera: Elegy for Young Lovers; The Bassarids
Instrumental
—orchestral

Karlheinz Stockhausen 1928-
Instrumental
—orchestral
—chamber
—solo
—electronic
—mixed medium

George Crumb 1929-
Vocal
—Night Music I and II (for soprano and chamber ensemble)
—Ancient Voices of Children (for voices and chamber ensemble)
—Madrigals (for voice and chamber ensemble)
Instrumental
—chamber: Black Angels (for electric string quartet)

Krystof Penderecki 1933-
Vocal
—opera: Devils of Loudon
—St. Luke's Passion (for solo voices, chorus and orchestra)
Instrumental—orchestral
—Threnody: to the Victims of Hiroshima (for string orchestra)

Morton Subotnick 1933-
Instrumental
—chamber
—electronic: Wild Bull
—mixed medium

Harrison Birtwistle 1934-
Vocal
Instrumental
—chamber

Mario Davidovsky 1934-
Instrumental
—electronic
—mixed medium: Synchronisms

Peter Maxwell Davies 1934-
Vocal
Instrumental
—orchestral
—chamber

Charles Wuorinen 1938-
Instrumental
—chamber
—electronic

Commentary

Stylistic Period Outline

This is an outline of the stylistic periods into which the works and composers in this guide are organized. There are six main chronologically arranged stylistic periods (Medieval through Modern) which are themselves divided into smaller sub-groups. The page numbers along the right hand margins locate each group on the Complete List and Commentary.

Map of Stylistic Periods

This chart shows the general relationships between the various stylistic periods and their sub-groups. Groups connected with a solid line indicates a strong stylistic similarity. A broken line indicates less similarity, while those groups with no line between them indicates little similarity. The direction of the arrow indicates the prevalent direction of influence. Thus, starting at the top of the chart, the French and Italian Ars Nova may be seen to be in a similar style, with the former largely influencing the latter. Continuing down, it can be seen that the early English Renaissance music is slightly similar to the French Ars Nova, and quite similar to the early Burgundian style.

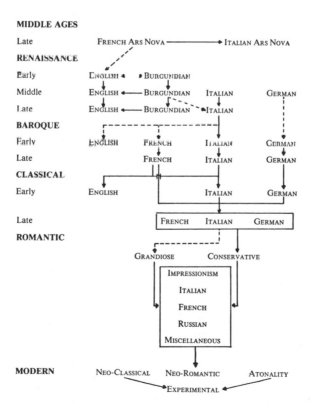

Commentary on Stylistic Periods

I. MEDIEVAL 500-1420

For the listener rather than the scholar or music historian the beginning of Classical music starts around the end of the Middle Ages with a style of music that was described in its own time as "Ars Nova"—a new art. Music before that time tends to sound too spare and somewhat crude and experimental for our ears.

A. CHANT 500-1100.

B. EARLY POLYPHONY 1100-1300.

see also
page 26

C. ARS NOVA 1300-1420.
There are two schools of Ars Nova music, one from France, the other from Italy. While the former is generally considered the most important, the difference between them is really only one of flavor.

To those who still think of the Middle Ages as a harsh, violent, generally crude and uncivilized time, the music of the late Middle Ages—the Ars Nova—will come as a shock. Ars Nova music is the antithesis of crudity. If anything it is over-refined. It is a delicate, precise, quiet, elegant music written to appeal to both the senses and the intellect. It is the apotheosis of courtly music. It is not at all dramatic. A better analogue than drama would be fine jewelry. There is no rush of excitement as climaxes approach, no sense of build, of pent up tension and final release. It is a music of delicate nuance and shading rather than broad gesture and violent contrast. All music may be said to be expressive. But if what is meant by that is the intense emotional display with which we often associate the music of, say, Beethoven, then the Ars Nova must be said to be an emotionally cool or impersonal music.

The primary medium of this music is the small instrumental ensemble supporting a solo voice. The short secular song—the chanson—is the forte of the style.

The ancient instruments needed to play this music along with its now obsolete technical structure go to create a sound which is always fascinating to modern ears, and often quite stunning.

II. RENAISSANCE 1420-1600

see also
page 27

A. EARLY 1420-1470. There are two main schools of early Renaissance music, the Burgundian (after the court of Burgundy, centered in the Netherlands) and the English. Technically there is little difference between them. Although the style originated with the English, the Burgundians brought it to its height—the latter is the better school.

The change from the Ars Nova to that of the early Renaissance is a large one, at first technical, then aesthetic. It is foremost a change in the sound itself (because of a dramatic shift in the overall harmonic structure), which gradually leads to a change in emotional effect. Early Renaissance music, like that of the Ars Nova, is delicate, refined, elegant. But where the latter is rather spare and open sounding, the music of the early Renaissance has a richer, warmer, less brittle sound. This move toward a more luxurious feel goes hand in hand with a general expansion of both the actual size and emotional scope of the music. While still not dramatic, there is a move away from the miniaturism of the Ars Nova toward a more spacious structuring. The fairly short instrumentally accompanied song—the chanson—is still a staple (especially in the hands of Dufay). But the broader and more stately church music, along with the use of the chorus, begins rapidly to grow in importance. The best pieces, though, are still the smaller ones—the secular chansons and shorter church pieces like the motets.

It is no exaggeration to say that in these pieces the early Renaissance saw some of the most finely wrought, sumptuously lyrical music ever written.

B. MIDDLE 1470-1560. From this period on, stylistic/national schools vary so much as to make it more practical to consider each individually. Burgundian music is the most important of this period.

1. Burgundian. Burgundian composers of the mid Renaissance quickly exploited the stylistic innovations of the previous generation to produce a music the scope and grandeur of which had yet to be known. Miniaturism, concentration on detail for its own sake, gives over in the mid Renaissance to a broad, often dramatic sweep. Choral music, unsupported by instruments, now becomes the central medium, a shift made possible by a general smoothing out of the musical texture. The sound is now one of long sinewy lines, intertwining and shearing off from one another. Music now soars as it has not since the days of Gregorian chant. The secular

see also
page 28

chanson is still important, but it is the longer, broader sacred music, especially the Mass and the now extended motet which takes precedence. This is still a refined, elegant and somewhat impersonal music. But with that refinement there is, at its best, an intensity which elevates this music to the level of the finest of the art of music as a whole.

see also page 30

2. ENGLISH. The English music of this period, though technically similar to that of the Burgundian school, is less advanced. It is in fact closer in scope to the music of the previous generation of Burgundian composers.

see also page 30

3. ITALIAN. Italian music sees the beginning of a style which will come to fruition in the next generation—the Italian madrigal.

see also page 30

4. GERMAN. Probably the most interesting German music of this period is the Lied, or song, which is in some sense the German counterpart to the French chanson. Like the chanson, it is sung with instrumental ensemble accompaniment. The Lied is generally more rhythmic and somewhat less refined in tone than the French chanson.

C. LATE 1560-1600. By the late Renaissance, music of the Italian as well as English schools began to vie seriously with that of the Burgundian in importance.

see also page 31

1. BURGUNDIAN. The Burgundian music of the late Renaissance is generally a refinement of the music of the previous generation. It is essentially the same style, but smoothed and polished even further.

see also page 31

2. ITALIAN. The Italian music of this period takes over the Burgundian musical language and adapts it to its own ends—ends which are the aesthetic antithesis of the Northern European school. Where Burgundian music is somewhat distant or abstract, Italian music, especially in the important secular madrigal, is warm and expressive—even passionate. The main stylistic difference is that the Italian school pays more attention to the text to which the music is set. The music not only tries to follow the rhythm of the words, thus producing a rhythmically livelier and more varied sound, but it tries to reflect the emotional content of the words as well. When the text speaks of a painfully unrequited love, the music expresses that torment—sometimes to the point of excessive mannerism. The madrigal of this period—the central form—is virtuoso music of the highest order, and is best performed with a small group of solo, unaccompanied voices.

3. ENGLISH.   English music of this period rises to a height which
it is never to surpass. The late Renaissance—the Elizabethan age—
is truly the golden age of English music. The central music of the
time is sacred, written in essentially the Burgundian style but with
the addition of a peculiarly English warmth. Almost as important
as the sacred music is the secular English madrigal, an amazing
mixture of Burgundian severity and Italian lightness, again, with a
distinctly English flavor. These pieces are a perfect companion to
the lyric poetry of the period. They can be humorous without
getting silly; or they can be profoundly serious without becoming
melodramatic. In the same vein as the English madrigal is the ex-
quisitely delicate lute song. A truly independent body of instrumental music also begins here first with pieces written for harpsichord and, second, in a style similar to the choral music, pieces for
viol consort (a precursor of the string quartet.)

see also
page 32

III. BAROQUE 1600-1750

The birthplace of the Baroque style is Italy, and Italy reigns
supreme almost throughout the period. In fact, the measure of the
"Baroqueness" of any of the music of this period is the degree to
which it becomes Italianette, and thus the general remarks here and
below on Baroque style can stand for a description of the Italian
Baroque as well. Germany may be considered the second most important country of the period, largely because of its adoption of
Italian practices, while England (with the single exception of Henry
Purcell) and France (with the exceptions of Jean Phillipe Rameau
and François Couperin), though producing some fine music in their
own rights, must be considered peripheral.

Although there are roots in the Italian music of the previous
generation, the Baroque style seems to spring suddenly from no-
where. It is as bold a stylistic shift as the history of music has ever
witnessed. The acute emotional tendencies of the Italian madrigal
of the previous generation are here institutionalized into the
dominant musical style with the results that the art of music as a
whole becomes hotter, more personal. It is as though immense
powers of expression and intensity are suddenly injected into the
musical language. All elements are effected—melody, harmony,
rhythm, even timbre and volume.

The smooth, even-paced, soaring language which dominated the
mid and late Renaissance now gives over to a tersely compressed
tense style with expressively dissonant harmonies, virtuostic colora-
tura melodies, and nervous, uneven rhythms. The cool, mono-

chromatic, chorally based sound and texture of the Renaissance is now variegated, polychrome.

Vocal music becomes predominantly solo vocal music—opera (a Baroque invention) is the quintessential form. Choral music is relegated to the church, a comparatively waning institution. All vocal music—choral and solo—is now instrumentally accompanied.

Independent instrumental music grows enormously in this period resulting in the establishment of the three main genres of instrumental music: orchestral, chamber and solo. The instruments themselves become louder and bigger, and become standardized into the categories which are familiar today: the violin group, the woodwind and brass groups and, the backbone of Baroque music, the keyboard instruments, the harpsichord and organ.

A. EARLY 1600-1700.   One effect of the violent stylistic debacle of the early Baroque period is that music fragmented into a plethora of styles and genres which can differ not only from country to country but from city to city as well. This plus the fact that each new generation of Baroque composers brought about various stylistic changes makes the early Baroque period a difficult one to capsulize. It is a period of great diversity.

see also
page 34
1. ITALIAN.   The central quality of the music of the early Italian Baroque is that of a restless, nervous, often aimless energy which effects not only the immediate sound of the music (in the form of agitated rhythms and expressively dissonant textures) but the overall shape as well. This music typically exchanges a broad architectural sweep for a more discursive, even halting movement, often with abrupt changes of mood. The elegance and restraint of the Renaissance is here traded for a more immediate, extrovert, emotional effect.

see also
page 36
2. GERMAN.   German music of the period is an often successful amalgam of the brilliant, expressive stylistic innovations of the Italian school with the denser, more complex style and texture indigenous to German music.

see also
page 37
3. ENGLISH.   English music of the period combines the intensity of expression of the Italian school with the voluptuousness of sound of the French to create a hybrid style which, with the exception of the strikingly beautiful, buoyant music of Henry Purcell, is often surprisingly bland.

see also
page 39
4. FRENCH.   For aesthetic as well as political reasons, the French consciously repelled the Italian influence in their music. The shift

from the Renaissance to Baroque styles in French music is similar in technical terms to the Italian shift, but the final effect is quite different. Where the Italians sought expressive and emotional effects, the French moved toward a more opulent and voluptuous, and yet restrained effect. France may indeed be said to have by-passed a truly Baroque style altogether, and proceeded directly to the Rococo or early Classical style described below.

Opera was central in France, but is generally too stylized and static for our tastes. More important to us is the instrumental music, especially the lush, delicate lute and harpsichord music.

B. LATE 1700-1750. In this period, primarily because of Bach and Handel, Germany is catapulted to center stage, where it is to remain for at least the next two centuries. Italian and German styles, however, are here nearly indistinguishable. France, with the exceptions of Rameau and Couperin, is of minor importance in this period, and England is virtually non-existent.

With the late Baroque we enter into what many regard as the golden age of classical music. Although the feeling is gradually changing (probably for the better), Bach and Handel, the titans of the Baroque period, are often considered the first truly great composers. However supreme they may be, though, certainly part of the credit for their success must be attributed to the development of the musical language with which they worked. By the end of the Baroque period, the musical language had gained a dimension of expression that was as significant to music as was the invention and control of visual perspective to the art of painting. The late Baroque style increased the breadth of the music of the previous generation while developing and controlling its expressive capabilities.

Rhythm becomes steadier and more forceful, melody and harmony more purposeful. The effect is, in the faster tempos, an almost mechanistically forceful, driving sound.

1. ITALIAN. For us the most important Italian music of this period is instrumental music, which the violin dominates. The central style is virtually identical to the of German music of the period. see also page 40

2. GERMAN. The late German Baroque is completely dominated by two of the most outstanding composers in the entire history of music, Johann Sebastian Bach and George Frideric Handel. see also page 41

Bach is the more serious of the two composers not only because he was largely a composer of sacred music (and was himself a deeply religious man) but because of his whole technical and aesthetic approach toward music. Bach's textures typically are complex and dense with intricate patterns and designs woven tightly into the fabric of his music. His music is virtuostic—but from the composer's rather than the performer's standpoint. Unlike many technically fine composers, Bach's skill translates perfectly into the sound, the effect of the music. Extraordinary compositional feats become extraordinary musical experiences. But what is most remarkable is the consistency of that skill. He was a master of the language of music in the same way that Shakespeare was a master of the language of words. No matter what the work or passage there is a continuously high level of intensity and virtuosity which almost never falters in Bach's music and which invariably astounds the careful listener.

Handel, by comparison, is a lighter composer. His textures are less thick and complex and his music tends toward the more theatrical style which would be expected from an opera composer. Handel's music seems more direct and outgoing, relying on a stirring melody, catchy rhythmic figure or well timed choral entrance for effect rather than the more intricate and subtle devices of Bach. The results are, at their best (as is well known from the famous examples from "The Messiah") overwhelming.

see also page 42 *3. FRENCH.* Jean-Philippe Rameau, the central figure of the late French Baroque, is famous as a music theorist as well as a composer of operas and harpsichord music. His music combines the richness of sound typical of French music of the period with a high sense of structuring. His operas, rather episodic in plot, abound in striking coloristic effects and share with the harpsichord works an imaginative and often bold approach toward harmony. The voluptuous, somewhat nervous opulence typical of the instrumental music of the previous generation is here continued and refined, particularly in the clavier music of François Couperin. The other French composers of the period are of minor importance.

IV. CLASSICAL 1725-1800

A. EARLY (ROCOCO) 1725-1775. The early Classical or Rococo style came about as a revolt against what was perceived as the heavy, indeed, ponderous style of the late Baroque. (The two styles co-existed—with Baroque on the decline and Classical on the rise—for at least 25 years). The result is a light, delicate sometimes frivolous music. Considering the immense success and importance of the two flanking periods (the late Baroque and the late Classical) it is almost impossible not to view this intermediate stage as a transitional period consisting of a hybrid style which probably found greatest (albeit limited) success in the music of the two Italian composers Domenico Scarlatti and Giovanni Battista Pergolesi.

1. GERMAN.   Compared to the German music of the previous generation, the style here displays a radical thinning of texture along with a loss of rhythmic drive. The kinetic enery of the late Baroque is dissipated and turned inward creating a music which, while aiming at a more immediate effect, seems shallow in comparison. The style is generally lighter, less complex, more discursive and short-winded. see also page 44

2. ENGLISH.   English music here, following the same trend as German music, makes little or no attempt to go beyond a rather tuneful, charming entertainment music. see also page 46

3. ITALY.   The two central composers of the early Classical period are the Italian composers Giovanni Battista Pergolesi and Domenico Scarlatti. see also page 47

   The music of Pergolesi maintains the driving rhythmic vitality of the late Baroque while adopting the thinner, leaner texture of the early Classical period. His opera "La Serva padrona" is famous not only for its central role in the polemic over the elaborate serious opera of the high Baroque and the new light comic "opera buffa" of which it is a prime example, but also for its intrinsic value as a lively, warm, brilliant bit of entertainment—in the best sense of the term.

   Scarlatti is exclusively known for his fiercely idiomatic harpsichord music. The virtuostic sparkle of the over 600 pieces he wrote for that instrument puts Scarlatti's works at the center of the harpsichordist's repertoire.

LATE 1750-1800.   Many consider the late Classical period to be the greatest in the entire history of music not only because of the three central composers of the period—Haydn, Mozart and Beethoven—but also because the musical language itself displays in this period what is perhaps the most perfect balance between the part and the whole, between content and form, that music has ever achieved. The late Classical style, when compared to either the late Baroque or Romantic styles seems simpler, less intense, even bland. Phrasing and rhythms are rather four-square, and harmony and melody seem somewhat too refined, too "pat." But this simplicity is only the "given" of the language. The greatness of the music of this period lies in the fact that the musical language itself is not expressive, but only potentially so. It is, like the language of words, an almost value-free or neutral language which, in the hands of a second rate artist, sounds flat and boring. But in the hands of a master, that neutrality acts as a stable reference point around which the composer can create his own dramatic perspective. The nature of the language, in other words, allows for great drama because it gives the composer room for contrast. And, more than any other music, it allows the drama to permeate throughout the entire work, to become part not only of the immediate content but of the whole structure. Thus the symphony, in the hands of a Classical composer has the greatest potential for becoming a powerfully unified dramatic form. But music of the Classical period is an easy music to misunderstand and become bored with because it is easy to let the refinement and conventionality of the musical language distract from the way that language is being used. If one listens beyond the surface of the music, however, late Classical music can be, at its best, incomparably expressive.

Instrumental music in all three categories of orchestral, chamber and solo flourish in this period. The piano here replaces the Baroque harpsichord as the central keyboard instrument. Opera is also important, as are, occasionally, sacred pieces with chorus and orchestra.

see also page 48 *1. GERMAN.*   German music is by far the most important of the late Classical period because of the great Classical triumvirate, Haydn, Mozart and Beethoven.

Haydn's most important contributions are in the symphony and the string quartet, both of which he is said, with some justification, to have invented. Living 77 years, he spanned the Classical period in its entirety. The whole of the development of the Classical style can be traced in his music alone. Thus, his earlier music displays the lighter, less expansive, less complex traits of the early Classical style, while his later music becomes more involved, and larger and deeper in scope and feeling. Although Haydn's music is generally lighter than either Mozart's or Beethoven's, and is often sprinkled with a buoyant humor and wit, it is a mistake to consider him anything less than one of the supreme geniuses of music whose range of expression is as great—and therefore as difficult to capsulize— as anyone's.

Mozart, the great *Wunderkind* of music who began composing at the age of six, is perhaps the subtlest of all the great composers and therefore the most difficult to readily appreciate. Though his music runs the gamut of expression, from the hilarious comedy of the opera "The Marriage of Figaro" to the overwhelming pathos of his Symphony #40 in G min., it never exceeds what the 18th century called "decorum." He is the only composer in all of music who was a complete master of both opera and instrumental music.

Beethoven, certainly the most famous and revered composer of all time, is in some ways the most accessible of the three great Classicists. This is partly because he, more than either Haydn or Mozart, anticipated the Romantic tendency to heighten the immediate effect of the musical language itself—the surface of his music conveys the same powerful message as does the whole piece. It is also due to the overtly dramatic character of his music—he is the master of the suspenseful build-up and the explosive release. His symphonies and piano sonatas stand at the center of his varied output.

2. FRENCH.   Except for the operas of Gluck, French music of the late Classical period is of minor importance. The dramatic sweep of German Classicism is generally diffused here by a less expressive but richer, more elegant feel. Operatic plotting is somewhat more stylized.

see also page 52

3. ITALIAN. The late Italian Classical music is similar in sound to the German music of the period, but is missing the imposing sense of structure.

see also page 52

V. ROMANTIC 1800-1900

There is no major stylistic shift from Classicism to Romanticism in music. The technical structure of music stays largely the same but is developed and expanded internally, resulting in a musical language which is much richer in feel, the surface or sound of which seems generally warmer and more expressive than the late Classical language, but which operates structurally in roughly the same manner. The result is a music which retains the essentially dramatic nature of the Classical language but which adds to it an element of passion or urgency. Thus, like the switch from the style of the Renaissance to that of the early Baroque (but to a lesser degree) the Romantic style as a whole seems hotter and more personal than that which preceded it. Sometimes in the Romantic period the dramatic element is minimized and the increased richness of the language is exploited for its own sake, resulting in a directly sensuous, lush, dream-like music.

The Romantic period sees a reversal in the trend toward unifying musical styles, toward the cosmopolitanism of the Classical period.

This is not just a result of the technical expansion of the musical language, but equally, a manifestation of the strong trend toward individualism in the Romantic period. The Romantic age is the era of the great Misunderstood Genius—the lone hero in possession of a nearly mystical insight into Truth and Beauty. All the arts, music included, become vehicles here for the expression of a highly personal vision. Thus music reflects more than ever the persona of its creator—be it the fiery extroversion of a Berlioz or the brooding melancholy of a Schubert—and so begins the trend toward the fragmentation of musical language or style into the countless individual languages and styles which is to become the earmark of 20th century music. Music from the Romantic period until the present becomes increasingly difficult to classify and characterize because of the increasing tendency for "music" to be overtaken by numerous separate "musics."

As far as the Romantic period proper, it is only partly true that the more conservative elements precede the more forward-looking ones. A more accurate picture is that there co-existed various schools of Romantic music simultaneously throughout the entire 19th century.

see also page 53
A. CONSERVATIVE.   The music of the Conservative Romantic school can be thought of as an extension of the Classical ideal of music as an autonomous, self-contained art form, but turned here toward the more subjective, expressive ends of the Romantic outlook. Instrumental music and the song (German Lied) are important here. Although the larger instrumental forms are used (e.g., the symphony and concerto), at least equally important are the shorter less expansive pieces (such as the character pieces for piano) because part of the aesthetic of the Conserative Romantics is that of self-expression on an intimate scale.

CARL MARIA VON WEBER is known only for a handful of fairly light works.

FRANZ SCHUBERT'S music, little known in his lifetime, tends to be introspective. It is in many ways the antithesis of virtuoso music. He is known for his chamber and piano works, a few orchestral pieces and, perhaps most of all, his over 600 songs.

FELIX MENDELSSOHN'S best music is often exuberant, outgoing, cheerful.

FRÉDÉRIC CHOPIN wrote almost exclusively for the piano and is considered the greatest composer for that instrument. He, like no one else, incorporated the idiomatic characteristics of the instrument into the music itself. The virtuostic skill needed to play much of his music, however, is never exploited for its own sake, but rather becomes an integral part of the nature and structure of the music itself.

ROBERT SCHUMANN, the articulate spokesman for the Conservative Romantic ideal, is known mostly for his piano music and songs and a few orchestral works.

JOHANNES BRAHMS, a student of Schumann's, is perhaps the greatest of the Conservative Romantics. While the emotional content of his music reaches the expressive limit of the Romantic ideal, his sense of structure, of form, seldom allows that content to turn inward and exhaust itself. He is a master of all three genres of instrumental music, orchestral, chamber and solo.

B. GRANDIOSE. In contrast to the Conservative school, the Grandiose Romantics broke entirely from the Classical ideal of restraint and poise. They believed in using any and all means to achieve their always highly subjective ends. The scope of this music is typically Gargantuan—symphonies using a thousand players and lasting well over an hour; operas several hours long; completely unrestrained virtuoso music (especially for the violin and piano). Although this category of Romantics includes such differing personalities as the introverted Mahler, the almost Classically detached Bruckner, and the great egoist Wagner, what unites them is the expanse of the canvas and palette they need to fulfill their tasks. This category of Romanticism tends to expand the Classically based language further than the Conservative, bending and stretching it almost beyond recognition to fit the expressive need. The result is often a highly chromatic, extremely restless, even orgiastic sound. The Grandiose Romantics were also the great orchestrators, the great colorists. The massive battery of percussion instruments and the huge brass choirs are part of the Grandiose Romantic palette.

see also page 57

HECTOR BERLIOZ was the great experimenter of the Grandiose Romantics. He achieved his generally extroverted expressive ends through a highly innovative approach to all aspects of music (form, orchestration, harmony, melody—everything) which can sound exhilarating to some ears but somewhat mannered to others. He is best known for his large orchestral works.

RICHARD WAGNER is known exclusively for his huge operas or music dramas in which the massive orchestra plays as central a role in the dramatic structure as does the singer on the stage. His only instrumental works of any consequence are orchestral excerpts from his operas, and his single chamber work, the "Sygfried Idyl."

FRANZ LISZT, famous in his day as an extraordinary virtuoso pianist, is best known for his aggressively extroverted orchestral and piano works. The accusation of "empty virtuosity" often leveled at him, though not totally unfounded, overlooks the expanse and diversity of his output.

ANTON BRUCKNER's music, though mammoth in conception, is generally more restrained than that of the other composers of the Grandiose Romantic school.

GUSTAV MAHLER used the full palette of the orchestra to create an intensely personal, introspective, yet almost theatrically dramatic music. His is a voluptuously lyrical music, the sprawling sense of form of which is countered not by restraint, but by a continuous flood of invention.

RICHARD STRAUSS' music runs the gamut from the violently expressive opera "Elektra" to the charming, ebullient tone poem "Till Eulenspiegel."

see also page 59 **C. IMPRESSIONISM.** The term "impressionism," borrowed from painting, is almost meaningless when applied to music—but it has, unfortunately, stuck. The musical impressionists extended the coloristic effects of the Grandiose Romantics and used the richness and variety of the sheer sound of music (whether timbral or harmonic) as an integral part of the musical language. Impressionism is thus typically anti-dramatic in the sense that the sound, the sensation, of the music itself becomes more important than the effect of movement.

see also page 61 **D. ITALIAN ROMANTICISM.** Italian music of the period consists mostly of opera. This is the age of Italian opera in its grandest, most dramatic, most popular—indeed archetypal—form. Both tragic and comic opera reach their zenith in this period.

see also page 62 **E. FRENCH ROMANTICISM.** French music of the period can be divided into two halves, early and late. The first half is dominated largely by the influence of Italian opera, and is of minor importance. Later French Romanticism, starting with Bizet, tends to fall midway between the Conservative and Grandiose schools, with Fauré nearer the former extreme and Saint-Saëns nearer the latter. French music of the period is often extravagant and tuneful, but rarely, except perhaps in the music of Fauré, reaching either the level of intensity or profundity found in either the Conservative or Grandiose schools.

see also page 65 **F. RUSSIAN.** Russian music of the period ranges from the fiery exuberance of Mussorgsky's "Night on Bald Mountain" to Borodin's plaintive "Polovetsian Dances" to the intensely expressive

Symphony #6 of Tchaikovsky. The best works of the period are typically brilliantly orchestrated, tuneful and, albeit perhaps a bit shallow, richly passionate.

G. MISCELLANEOUS.   Including such disparate compositions as the light, indeed, giddy works of Offenbach to the lush extravagances of Grieg to the brooding miniatures of Hugo Wolf, this frankly catch-all category illustrates the increasing tendency of the Romantic period toward the individualism which makes codification virtually impossible in some cases. see also page 67

VI. MODERN 1900-Present

There is a school of thought that good listenable music ceased with the death of Brahms. Although this is, of course, an absurd view, only the most fiercely partisan supporter of modern music would insist that the quality of art music as a whole has not declined somewhat in the 20th century. There are numerous aesthetic, cultural and sociological reasons for this, but certainly one of the most important reasons is purely technical.

Music since the beginning of the Classical period through the end of the Romantic is all based on essentially the same structural principles. The differences in styles from generation to generation and composer to composer amount to differences in the *treatment* of this same basic language, not differences in the language itself. Many believe that by the beginning of the 20th century, this basic language got "used up." Its viability as an adequate artistic language became exhausted. How could this be? It is not a difficult view to understand itf it is recognized that the fundamental necessary element of any musical language is that of internal contrast. The essential affect of all music is motion and motion is gained in music through the contrast of the effect of tension vs. relaxation. If a musical language gets so dense or complex that a clear contrast between tension and relaxation—dissonance and consonance—is no longer perceivable then it loses its power to create the illusion of motion. This is basically what happened by the end of the 19th century. And it partly explains why much of the music of the time is so tortuously expressive: It needs to be if it is to work at all. Subtlety can only work if the medium used to convey it is sufficiently sensitive.

There are those, then, who see the 20th century as music's painful final days. But these critics forget that this is not the first time that a musical language has been "used up." The ends of the

14th and 16th centuries both saw a similar "crisis." And both were followed by bold new experiments that eventually lead to music of unimaginable greatness.

The 20th century is just such an age of experimentation. It is a time when composers are burdened with an absolute freedom concerning not only the materials of their art, but the beliefs about it as well. What is music? What should it do? What are its limits? What is the proper relationship between music of the past and that of the present? What is good music? Who is to judge? Is there any standard at all? These questions and thousands like them are what face the composer—as well as the listener—in the 20th century.

From the listener's standpoint 20th century music can often be a frustrating experience. But it can be an exciting and rewarding one as well. Listening to modern music is sometimes more strenuous than listening to music of earlier times, not only because of its newness and, often, complexity, but also because the judgement of history has not yet removed from us the burden of evaluating for ourselves what we hear. But these difficulties shouldn't discourage one from exploring modern music, from facing the challenge of discriminating, in one's own mind, between what is genuine and what is sham, between what is truly eloquent and merely startling or diverting. For modern music offers us something that music of no other time can. Ourselves. It speaks to us with a vitality, an urgency, an immediacy that no other music is capable of. For, like it or not, it is as much a part of us as are our television sets and airplanes and car washes. It is true that we can, as many do, turn our backs on modern music, ignore it, wholly dismiss it. But what we gain in comfort we lose in growth. New music offers us new experiences. And though they can often be trying ones, they can also be exhilarating and moving. That is they, ultimately, can be musical.

Of course not all music in the 20th century is difficult. In fact, one of the problems in dealing with modern music is its diversity. The trend toward the atomization of musical styles which started at the beginning of the Romantic period continues even to the present day, making contemporary music virtually impossible to adequately capsulize. For this reason, the stylistic groups of the Modern period must be understood as being even more provisional than those of the earlier periods. Few if any modern composers fit into any simple category easily.

see also
page 71 **A. NEO-CLASSICAL.** The Neo-Classical school of modern music—so named because of the supposed antipathy toward the attitudes of Romantic self-expression as well as a rather superficial

adoption of some of the formal schemes of the music of the Classical period—consists of numerous diverse styles and types of music. What unites them generally is an approach to music which, while throwing out many of the technical rules of the "traditional" music of the Classic/Romantic language, it attempts, at the same time, to achieve roughly the same ends as does that earlier music. The result is often an unusual sounding music, but one which succeeds affectively in the same way as does that earlier music.

BELA BARTOK often incorporated in his music elements of the folk music of his native Hungary, giving it a rather exotic sound. His music, in the faster tempos, can be fiercely percussive and biting, while at slower speeds, it can be strangely hauntingly effective.

PAUL HINDEMITH, known as both a theorist and a composer wrote such an enormous amount of music that, considering the degree of stylistic freedom he had, it is no wonder that it varies greatly in quality. His best works display a completely novel and successful approach to melody and, in particular, harmony. It is never too difficult to recognize the clean, angular, "Germanic" sound of Hindemith's polished and often dramatically moving music.

FRANCIS POULENC's music is in many ways typically French —witty, ironic, elegant—and perhaps at times a bit over-refined. His dynamic colorful choral works are among his finest pieces.

IGOR STRAVINSKY. Many people consider the Russian composer Stravinsky to be the last great composer—a view which is not easy to ignore. Certainly he stands at the center of the Neo-Classical school as not only the greatest composer of that group, but as its most influential one as well. Such works as his Rite of Spring, the Symphony of Psalms and the Octet for Winds are as likely candidates for future survival as any that can be thought of. Though his music is often brutal in its expressive force, it is usually tempered and controlled by an elegance and wit learned from the French Neo-Classicists of the time. Stravinsky's earlier music is in the archetypal Neo-Classical style, but later he adopted the stylistic techniques of the atonalists.

BENJAMIN BRITTEN may be said to have constituted a one-man renaissance of English music. His best known and best works are his highly dramatic yet beautifully written operas. While using many of the technical devices of the Neo-Classical school, his music tends to lie more in the aesthetic tradition of Romanticism.

AARON COPLAND's music, like Britten's, uses Neo-Classical devices for essentially Romantic ends. The earmarks of Copland's music are a lush opulent sound and texture combined with engaging catchy rhythms and melodies.

DMITRI SHOSTAKOVICH, the Soviet composer, tends to write extremely dramatic music, romantic in tone.

OLIVIER MESSIAEN, the French teacher, organist, and composer, like Hindemith, has written a lot of music of varying quality. His best works, like his early masterpiece, Quartet for the End of Time (written and first performed in a Nazi POW camp), are deeply passionate and sincere. Although his music sometimes tends to ramble, his novel approach to rhythm, melody, and harmony makes usually for a fascinating listening experience.

see also
page 75

B. NEO-ROMANTIC. The Neo-Romantic composers carry on the tradition of late 19th century Romanticism, often employing, however, some of the technical devices invented by the Neo-Classicists. In fact, it is impossible to draw a firm line between these schools—one simply melds into the other.

see also
page 78

C. ATONALITY. Atonality (see Glossary) came about as a result of the belief that the language of "traditional" music was dead or dying and that something new had to be tried. Numerous composers, most notably Schoenberg, experimented with various ideas, trying first to understand how traditional music worked, and then determining how to accomplish that same end via new means. The success of the experiments in these terms is debatable; but what is not debatable is that the efforts of these composers raised numerous questions about music and the way it worked which eventually resulted in what many regard as a musical crisis. Although the works of the atonalists often seem unbearably harsh to new listeners, it is wrong to dismiss them all out of hand as "unmusical." New ideas never come easily, and we must constantly remind ourselves that the path of the history of all art is strewn with verdicts of condemnation which were later themselves proven wrong.

The great triumvirate of the early atonalists were the three Viennese composers, Schoenberg, Berg and Webern. Each of these three members of the "New Viennese" school knew and was influenced by the other.

ALBAN BERG's music is generally the most accessible of the three. It is less severe in both its application of theoretical constraints as well as in its expressive aims. Many consider his "Wozzeck" to be the only true operatic masterpiece of the 20th century.

ANTON WEBERN is generally considered the least accessible of the three prime members of the "New Viennese" school. His propensity for devising and rigidly applying complex theoretical constructs sometimes makes his music close to impossible to enjoy from a purely aural standpoint. Formal rigidity, spareness to the point of bleakness, and extreme brevity are all to be found in Webern's music. Not all his works, however, are this severe. At its most listenable his music, while rarely warm, can be intriguing and quite lovely.

ARNOLD SCHOENBERG's early works are in the same general style as his mentor's, Gustave Mahler. Soon, however, under the influence of the artistic and literary movement of Expressionism, he began rapidly expanding the expressive capabilities of the Romantic musical language, achieving a highly mannered, emotionally supercharged, tense style of music. Eventually he sought to control this style via his invention of the 12-tone method of composition (see Serialism in the Glossary) wherein every note of a work is subject to certain strict formal constraints. Even at the peak of his Expressionist and Serialist styles, Schoenberg's music betrays the Romantic foundation of his aesthetic, which no matter how extreme his music may become, always keeps his music within the bounds of what the art of music has always meant.

D. EXPERIMENTAL. Like the Miscellaneous category of Romanticism, this catch-all category includes composers of extremely diverse output and who simply defy classification. Each composer in this section embodies a separate solution to the problem of 20th century music.

see also page 80

Appendix

On Buying Records
Glossary of Terms
Bibliography of Books on Music
Composers' Index

On Buying Records

Because of the large number of classical recordings and the diversity in quality between them, buying classical records can be difficult. As with so many things, once you have begun you can find your way around well enough, but getting started can be a problem. The following is designed to help the new buyer.

The first thing to know about is the *Schwann* catalog of tapes and records. It comes out every month and lists most of the available classical records in print. It is available for use or purchase in most record stores.

So, having determined what is available, how does one choose? What is the criteria for a good classical recording and how does one find one?

First off, there are two factors to consider in a classical recording: 1) the quality of the recorded sound itself, and 2) the quality of the performance. Both of these figure in the final listening experience.

As regards the first point, just how important good quality sound is to you is a matter of individual taste. Whereas some can't tolerate anything short of an almost perfectly reproduced sound, others are willing to put up with terrible sound quality in order to hear a superior performance. Unfortunately, good sound and a good performance do not necessarily go hand in hand.

In terms of the second point, the quality of performance, it has to be admitted that there is much room for disagreement as to what makes a good performance of any given piece. However, there are minimum standards of quality about which most would agree. And it is not true that because you are not an experienced listener, or that you have not heard the piece before that the quality of the performance will not matter. In fact, the opposite is true, because without familiarity with the piece or the music as a whole, it is difficult to distinguish between the quality of the piece itself and the quality of the performance of it. A boring performance of an exciting piece will result in a boring listening experience.

With these points in mind, how does the new buyer ensure at least minimally good recording and performance quality?

The classical record industry is separated into two main divisions, budget records and regular-priced records. Although it may be tempting to begin exploring classical music via budget labels, it is wiser for the beginner to stick to the major regular-priced labels. (Some are listed below). Although this is no absolute guaranty of quality, it is probable that really poor sound and performances will be avoided this way. Even though most budget labels are subsidiaries of major regular-priced label companies, the discrepancy in quality of budget records makes them a risky buy for the newcomer. Saving a couple of dollars for a terrible recording is no bargain. Budget records can be an excellent buy, but only if you know what you are doing.

Beyond this general rule of thumb, a good way to find quality records is through record reviews such as those in *High Fidelity* and *Stereo Review* magazines. A helpful item is the "Basic Repertoire" list offered free by *Stereo Review* which recommends over 150 recordings of basic works. Information about this yearly updated list can be found in any issue of that magazine. Other useful items are the yearly compilations of record reviews published in book form. There are several of these offered by different publishers and can be purchased at some record stores or through book stores.

Perhaps the easiest way to find good recordings is simply to ask the clerk in your record store for recommendations. If the store carries a fairly large selection of classical records, there will usually be someone who knows the stock well and will be able to make suggestions.

There is, of course, no way to ensure that every classical recording you buy will be all that you hoped for. Such is the case with records of any category. But what makes the classical record a particularly good buy is that the recordings which *are* good, which *do* live up to your expectations, will never grow old. They will not fade with the current musical fashion. A fine classical recording is, literally, a thing of joy forever.

Some major regular-priced record labels are:
  Angel
  Archiv
  Columbia
  Deutsche Grammophon
  EMI
  London
  Oiseau-Lyre
  Phillips
  RCA
  Seraphim
  Telefunken

Glossary of Terms

A CAPELLA. A descriptive term for choral music without instrumental accompaniment.

ANTHEM. A type of choral composition in English similar to the late Baroque German cantata*. The form flourished in England from the late Renaissance to the late Baroque.

ATONALITY. A system of pitch organization (or rather, a non-system) wherein no pitch or group of pitches dominates or subordinates other pitches as in tonally* organized pitches. Atonality is often associated with serialism* and various forms of avant-garde music. (See p. 104)

BALLADE. 1. One of the standard forms of the French chanson* of the 14th century. 2. a 19th century character piece*.

BARCAROLE. A Venetian gondolier's boatsong, or imitation thereof, often in the form of a character piece*.

BI- tonality. The simultaneous existence of two tonal* centers in a work. Like poly-tonality* this technique was used by numerous composers during the first half of the 20th century.

BI-TONALITY. The simultaneous existence of two tonal* centers in a work. Like poly-tonality* this technique was used by numerous composers during the first half of the 20th century, especially those of the Neo-Classical school. (See p. 102). Stravinsky used this technique often. See "tonality."

CADENCE. An harmonic or melodic formula which is used to close a musical phrase.

CADENZA. A brief musical passage either improvised or in an improvisational style inserted typically near the end of a composition, suspending the forward motion of the piece, and giving the performer a chance to exhibit his virtuostic skill.

CANON. A compositional device similar to a round wherein a melody is begun and joined by a duplication of itself.

* = see other entry.

CANTATA. A form of vocal music used in the Baroque period. It originated in Italy c. 1600 as a small secular form for solo voice with instrumental accompaniment in several short sections. The better known type of cantata is the later German Baroque cantata typical of J. S. Bach, which is a sacred work lasting about thirty minutes consisting of vocal solos, duets, and/or choruses with orchestral accompaniment in sections of various length.

CANTUS FIRMUS. The "given," pre-existent melody on which a polyphonic* composition is sometimes based. The use of a cantus firmus as a basis for composition was common in the Renaissance.

CAPRICCIO. A type of 19th century character piece* of a capricious or humorous flavor.

CEMBALO. A harpsichord.

CHACONNE. A type of variation* composition used mostly in the Baroque period. The Passacaglia is a similar form.

CHAMBER MUSIC. Instrumental ensemble music which is performed by one player to a part (as opposed to orchestral music which is played by several players to a part).

CHANSON. French for song. The French counterpart to the German Lied*. The most important periods of the French chanson are 1) the monophonic* chanson of the troubadors and trouveres of the later Middle Ages, 2) the polyphonic* chanson of the later Middle Ages and Renaissance, and 3) the 19th century chanson for voice and piano, of which Gabriel Fauré is the prime exponent.

CHANT. See plainchant.

CHARACTER PIECE. The generic term for a fairly short, one movement, instrumental piece (usually for the piano) in the 19th century, often expressing a single mood or idea. Such specific titles as Intermezzo, Ballade, Songs without Words (Mendelssohn), Impromptu (Schubert), Prelude (Chopin and Debussy) etc. are often used.

CLAVICHORD. A small keyboard instrument used in the Baroque and early Classical periods. Like the piano, it uses hammers to strike the strings, but is much quieter than either the piano or the harpsichord.

CLAVIER. A generic term used in the Baroque period for any keyboard instrument (harpsichord, clavichord*, organ, etc.)

COLLEGIUM MUSICUM. A term now used to signify a group of

musicians typically attached to a university, who specialize in performing pre-Classical music.

CONCERT MASTER. The first violinist of an orchestra.

CONCERTO. A form of instrumental music in use since the Baroque period wherein a solo or group of solo instruments play with and are contrasted against an orchestra. "Concerto grosso" is the term for the type of Baroque concerto which uses a group of soloists as opposed to just one. (J. S. Bach's "Brandenburg Concertos" are famous examples). In later periods when there were two (three) soloists the term double (triple) concerto was used. From the Classical period through the Romantic the schematic form of the concerto followed that of the symphony*.

CONCERTO GROSSO. See concerto.

CONSONANCE/DISSONANCE. See harmony.

CONSORT. Originally a 17th century term for an instrumental chamber ensemble, it is now usually used to designate a performing ensemble specializing in Renaissance or Medieval music.

CONTINUO. The name of the figured bass* part in a Baroque composition.

CONTRAPUNTAL. See counterpoint.

COUNTERPOINT. A type of music consisting of the simultaneous combination of two or more melodies. Also called polyphony.

DA CAPO ARIA. An ABA aria in which the second "A" is not written out. The form was popular in the Baroque opera where it was assumed that the second "A" would be ornamented* by the singer.

DEVELOPMENT. The technique of re-using material within a work in various ways. The center section of the first movement of the Classical symphony* is called the development section because it develops material laid out in the opening section. The techniques of development run from such simple devices as repetition of phrases to such complex procedures as the subtle transformations and re-combination of motifs* and themes. Beethoven and Brahms are considered masters of musical development.

DEVELOPMENT SECTION. See development.

DIES IRAE. A particular Gregorian chant* and text used in the Requiem Mass*. The Dies irae text was sometimes set to new music by later composers (e.g., Mozart and Verdi) and the melody was sometimes used as the basis for new instrumental works (e.g., Berlioz' "Symphonie fantastique.")

DIVERTEMENTO. A generic name used often in 18th century Austria to designate a fairly light type of instrumental work in a variety of forms.

DOUBLE CONCERTO. See concerto.

ELECTRONIC MUSIC. Generally, any music produced electronically. The term, however, is often used to designate a type of 20th century music in which electronically produced (or altered) sounds are used as the fundamental building blocks of music rather than the more conventional material of pitch.

ETUDE. A type of instrumental piece designed as an exercise for a particular problem in performance technique. Chopin's Etudes for piano are fine examples of the form.

FIGURED BASS. A shorthand method of musical notation used in the Baroque period for an accompanying keyboard part wherein only the bass note is written down and the rest of the notes to be played are either implied by the context or are suggested by a conventional system of numbers (figures) provided by the composer. The overwhelming majority of Baroque orchestral and chamber works have a part for figured bass called the continuo part.

FUGUE. A strict contrapuntal* form of music which uses a short melody called a "subject" as the kernel from which the entire work grows. The fugue is considered the most difficult form to handle successfully. J. S. Bach's fugues, which are often preceded by shorter freer preludes, are the apotheosis of the form. Although fugues are often written as independent works, the term "fugue" signifies not as much an independent form as a way of writing, a treatment of voices*. Thus, fugues are often incorporated into larger forms, such as sonatas* or symphonies*.

GAVOTTE. A 17th century French dance in moderate 4/4 time often used in Renaissance and Baroque suites*.

GIGUE. A quick dance in triple time often used as the finale in Renaissance and Baroque suites*.

GREGORIAN CHANT. The name of a body of plainchant* used in the Catholic church. Its name comes from Pope Gregory I (The Great) who helped standardize the music of the church in the ninth century. Although sometimes used as a generic term for all types of monophic* chant, Gregorian chant is actually only a specific body of plainchant.

HARMONY. Generally, the phenomenon of two or more pitches sounded simultaneously. Harmony is often divided into the two affective categories of consonance and dissonance. The difference between the two types has to do with the perceived degree of "tension" created by the harmony. Tension is here a relative term in the sense that all harmonic configurations can be matched with other configurations that are comparatively less or more tense. Thus, depending on the context as a whole (that is, the harmonic system in use) a given harmony may be considered dissonant in one context and consonant in another. The history of musical harmony is the history of these changing contexts. One of the central issues of 20th century music is the degree to which and the speed with which the human ear can adapt to new harmonic systems and contexts.

INCIDENTAL MUSIC. Music to accompany a play.

INTERMEZZO. 1. A kind of character piece*. 2. A short, light vocal work written to be performed between the acts of an opera, especially popular in the Baroque period.

INTERVAL. The distance (measured in ratios of pitch frequency) between either successive or simultaneous pitches (called melodic and harmonic* intervals, respectively).

INVENTION. A term used by Bach to signify certain fugue*-like compositions of his.

KEY. See tonality.

KEY SIGNATURE. See tonality.

LIED. German for song. As with the French chanson*, there are three main periods and therefore styles of Lied: 1) The monophonic Lied of the Minnesingers and Meistersingers, c. 1250-1500, 2) the polyphonic Lied of the Renaissance, and 3) the "German Lied" of the 19th century for solo voice with piano accompaniment, composed mostly by German composers of the Conservative Romantic school. Franz Schubert is generally considered the greatest master of the German Lied.

LIETMOTIF. A motif* used throughout a work for formal or dramatic purposes. The term is often associated with the operas of Wagner in which the lietmotif is often used as an integral part of the structure.

MADRIGAL. 1. A 14th century secular Italian form of instrumentally accompanied solo vocal music, analogous to the French chanson* of the same period. 2. A kind of 16th century secular

Italian unaccompanied vocal music sung by several voices, one to a part.

MAGNIFICAT. A scriptural text of 12 verses (beginning "Magnificat anima mea Dominum"—My soul doth magnify the Lord) used in the Office* of the Vespers in the Roman Catholic church. The text was set to music by countless composers, especially from the 15th to the 18th centuries.

MAJOR/MINOR. See tonality.

MASS. The central service of the Roman Catholic church. It is divided into two alternating parts: the Proper whose text varies from day to day, and the Ordinary whose text stays the same for every Mass. Both parts of the Mass have sections set to music which were sung in plainchant*. In the 14th century, however, composers began the thus far unbroken tradition of writing new music for the Mass, especially for the stable Ordinary portion. When one refers to a musical setting of a Mass, it almost always means a setting of the five main parts of the Ordinary, the Kyrie, Gloria, Credo, Sanctus, and Agnus Dei. Machaut's Mass in the Middle Ages, Dufay's "Se la face ay pale" in the Renaissance, Bach's B minor Mass in the Baroque period, Beethoven's Mass in D in the Classical period and Verdi's Requiem Mass in the Romantic period are all famous examples.

MAZURKA. A Polish dance in triple time varying in tempo from rather slow to very quick. Chopin's Mazurkas for piano are famous examples.

METER. A fixed pattern of beats in music, such as 3/4 (one, two, three, one, two, three, etc.) and 4/4 (one, two, three, four, one, two, three, four, etc.) specified in musical notation by the time signature.

MINOR/MAJOR. See tonality.

MISSA. Latin for Mass.

MODULATION. See tonality.

MONODY. Although sometimes used as a synonym for monophony* the term refers more correctly to a type of early 17th century Italian song for solo voice with keyboard accompaniment in recitative* style.

MONOPHONY. A single unaccompanied melody.

MOTET. Generally, a vocal composition on a sacred though not liturgical text. The term originated around 1220 to signify musical works created by adding new words to pre-existing music. ("Mot" is French for "word." Soon, however, newly composed pieces written in a style similar to these were also called motets. As the motet has existed continuously from the Middle Ages to the present day, and has seen as many changes as there have been generations of composers, it is impossible here to accurately describe "The Motet." From the Renaissance on, however (when it was the central form of music along with the Mass*), the motet is almost always a choral piece of moderate length, often in several sections.

MOTIF, or motive. The smallest recognizable melodic idea, typically from two to four notes long. Motifs are often used throughout a piece or section thereof as a unifying element. (See Leitmotif). The opening four note figure of the Beethoven 5th Symphony is probably the most famous motif in all of music.

MOVEMENT. See symphony.

NEO-CLASSICISM. See p. 102.

OBBLIGATTO. Italian for obligatory. Usually the term refers to an instrumental or vocal part in a piece of music which must be played. It sometimes means, however, just the opposite—that the part so marked may be omitted.

OCTET. A group of eight instruments or a piece written for such a group. There is no standard octet grouping.

ODE. In English Renaissance and Baroque music a secular Anthem*.

OFFICES, THE DIVINE. The eight daily services (apart from the Mass*) of the Roman Catholic church. Matins (held usually between midnight and dawn), Vespers (sunset), Lauds (sunrise), and Compline (immediately after Vespers) are musically the most important. Vespers in particular (which includes the Magnificat*) was often set to elaborate music especially during the Baroque period. Monteverdi's Vespers of 1610 is perhaps the most famous example.

OPUS. Literally, "work." The opus number of a piece of music labels the work and often signifies the chronology of publication. Op. 1, for example, would be an early work, while Op. 100 would be a later one. Beethoven (born 1772) was the first composer to use opus numbers fairly consistently in this fashion. Often, however, early works are published at a later date and so appear with misleadingly high opus numbers. Several works may have one opus number, such as in many of Haydn's quartets, for example,

Op. 76, #s 1-6. Often the initial of a scholar who has ordered the works of a composer is used instead of opus numbers (as in the music of Mozart and Schubert). In this case whether a number signifies chronological placement of the work depends on the system of organization used. Kochel (K.) numbers of Mozart, for example, do generally signify chronology whereas Pincherele (P.) numbers for Vivaldi do not.

OPUS POSTHUMUS. A work published after a composer's death.

ORATORIO. A long work for chorus, solo singers, and orchestra usually on a sacred text. Handel's "Messiah" is probably the best known oratorio in all music.

ORNAMENTATION. The usually improvised musical figuration a performer adds to a given piece. Baroque music especially was written with the assumption that performers would add ornaments to it.

OSTINATO. A continuously repeated melodic figure.

OVERTURE. Generally, an orchestral composition intended as an opening to an opera, ballet, etc. The early overtures in the Baroque period were in no specific form. By the 19th century overtures were being written as completely independent orchestral works, usually modelled on the same plan as the first movement of a symphony* (as, for example, the "Academic" and "Tragic" overtures of Brahms).

PASSACAGLIA. See chaconne.

PAVANE. A slow 16th century dance in 4/4 time which was popular in a stylized fashion with many composers of the English late Renaissance. It is often followed by a faster dance like the Galliard.

PEDAL POINT. A long sustained note typically in the bass.

PHILHARMONIC. A symphony orchestra.

PIANO QUARTET. See quartet.

PIANO TRIO. See trio.

PLAINCHANT or plainsong. The generic term for the monophonic* vocal music of the early Christian church. Although sometimes used as a synonym for Gregorian chant*, the latter is really only a type of plainchant, as are Ambrosian chant, Byzantine chant, and Mozarabic chant.

POLYPHONY. Literally, many voices. A more general term for counterpoint*, which tends to imply a certain type of polyphony.

POLYTONALITY. The simultaneous existence of two or more tonal* centers in a piece of music. This rather short-lived technique was employed by numerous composers during the first half of the 20th century, especially those of the Neo-Classical school. Darius Milhaud was perhaps the prime exponent of the technique. See bitonality and tonality.

PRELUDE. Until the 19th century, any piece, usually fairly short, written as an introduction to something else. In the 19th century, the term was used to stand for a non-specific type of character piece*.

PROGRAM MUSIC. Music based on, and often illuminating, some extramusical idea or "program." Debussy's "La Mer" (The Sea) is a famous example. "Absolute music" is a term used as the opposite of program music (that is, non-programmatic music). "Tone poem" and "symphonic poem" are terms often used to designate orchestral program music on a rather specific program, such as Richard Strauss' "Don Quixote" and "Don Juan."

QUARTET. A group of four instruments or voices or music for such a group. The string quartet usually consists of two violins, a viola, and a cello. Other types of quartets, such as the piano quartet (for three strings and a piano) are less standardized.

QUINTET. A group of five instruments or voices, or music for such a group. The string quintet, though less standardized than the string quartet*, usually consists of two violins, two violas, and a cello. The piano quintet (as the clarinet quintet, etc.) is usually for string quartet and piano (clarinet, etc.)

RECITATIVE. A style of vocal music wherein the rhythm and word declamation lie halfway between a rather agitated speech and music. It is used frequently between the arias of operas in order to accelerate the plot.

REQUIEM. The Roman Catholic Mass* for the dead.

RICERCARE. A precursor of the fugue*.

RONDEAU. One of the standard forms of the Medieval and Renaissance French chanson*.

SCHERZO. 1. The third movement of many symphonies in fast 3/4 time and rather robust rhythm. (See minuet). 2. A dramatic type of character piece*. Chopin's Scherzos are the most famous.

SEPTET. A group of seven instruments or voices, or music for such a group. There is no standard septet ensemble, but the most common is a mixture of strings and woodwinds.

SERIALISM. A system of pitch organization devised largely by Arnold Schoenberg in the early part of the 20th century in order to compensate for the disintegration of the tonal* system of pitch organization in music, which he perceived was taking place during his generation. The fundamental idea is that a composer writes a "series" of 12 pitches (necessarily using all 12 tones of the chromatic scale—thus the term 12-tone music) to be used as the seed from which the entire composition must grow. In its strictest form all the notes in the piece, whether melodic or harmonic, must derive from this unbroken series, also called a tone row. The composer's freedom lies not only in the creation of the row itself, but in the manipulation of it as well.

The theoretical and practical relationship between serialism and tonality is unclear. It is one of the implicit tenets of serialism that for the system to work, the composer must consciously abolish any sense of tonality. Serialism, however, does not by definition exclude tonal organization, yet serially organized tonality seems superfluous. Numerous works though (for example, certain pieces by Alban Berg and Luigi Dallapiccola), clearly exist in both tonal and serial worlds. It is also unclear whether serial organization is at all an equivalent replacement for the tonal system.

Many composers during Schoenberg's lifetime began to adopt serialism, and it has, in fact, become a staple of the modern composer's compositional technique. (See p. 104).

SEXTET. A group of six instruments or voices or music for such a group. There is no standard sextet grouping.

SINFONIA. 1. Italian for symphony. 2. A term used by Bach for his three part inventions*. 3. During the Baroque period, a synonym for overture.

SONATA. Generally, the name of a type of instrumental composition. Before the Classical period (1725-1800), the history of the term "sonata" is extremely varied and complex. Around 1750, however, the sonata, like the symphony, evolved into its archetypal form—the composition for solo instrument (piano, or violin, clarinet, etc. with piano accompaniment) in three or four movements, similar in layout to that of the Classical symphony*.

SONG CYCLE. A group of songs designed to constitute a single musical entity. Schubert's song cycles are perhaps the most famous and greatest examples of the form.

SUITE. A group of musical dances designed to be performed as a single entity. The suite was a popular form in the Renaissance and Baroque periods. There is some debate as to whether certain suites were actually meant to be danced to, but it is clear that many (as for example those of J.S. Bach) were not.

SYMPHONIC POEM. See program music.

SYMPHONY. A form of orchestral music which grew from several sources in the late Baroque/early Classical period. The symphonic form became standardized in the Classical period, particularly through the efforts of F. J. Haydn. The archetypal classical symphony consists of four self-contained sections called movements. The first movement, usually in a fast tempo, is typically in what is called a "sonata" or "sonata-allegro" form which consists of three large sections called the 1) exposition (in which all the material is presented), 2) the development* (in which that material is developed), and 3) the recapitulation (in which the material of the exposition is played again). The second movement is usually in a slow tempo in a variety of forms. The third movement is usually a minuet or trio which is a kind of stylized minuet (a dance in 3/4 time in moderate tempo) with a contrasting middle section. The last movement, the finale, is usually in fast tempo and, like the second movement, in a variety of forms.

From the beginning of the Romantic period (1800-1900), the symphony begins to lose its standard shape until the end of the 19th century when the term can stand for almost any large orchestral piece.

SYMPHONY ORCHESTRA. A large orchestra.

SYNTHESIZER. Generally, a device designed to produce sounds electronically. The term usually refers to the elaborate devices built specifically for the purpose of creating electronic music*.

TE DEUM. A Gregorian chant* text of praise (used usually at the Office* of Matins) beginning "Te deum, laudamus" (We praise thee, O Lord). The Te deum text has been set countless times by composers, especially since the 17th century, when it began to be used as a hymn for special celebrations of all kinds.

THOROUGH-BASS. See figured bass.

THROUGH COMPOSED. A type of musical form containing no formal repetition. The term is usually applied to songs which have new music for each new stanza of text.

TIMBRE, or tone color. The aural nature or quality of any sound or tone. Thus, the difference between the sounds of a middle C pitch played on a flute, a trumpet, and a violin is one of timbre.

TIME SIGNATURE. See meter.

TOCCATA. A typically free-form composition for keyboard instrument in an idiomatic style.

TONALITY. 1. Generally, the principle of pitch organization wherein a single pitch subordinates all others in a given work or section. Thus, in tonal music all pitches tend toward the central pitch, called the "tonic" note. The tonic note is thus the most stable pitch and is therefore often the last note of a work, phrase, or section. The overwhelming majority of music, whether classical, popular, or folk, is tonal in this sense.

2. The term tonality also refers to a rather specific system of tonality as defined above. This system, sometimes called the "major/minor" system of tonality, or the "common practice" system, involves the ordering not only of pitch, but of the harmonic* aspect of pitch as well, in such a way as to give virtually every harmonic combination and melodic note a particular identity in terms of its relation to the system as a whole. Thus, any given note or harmony in a work based on the common practice system of tonality has a specific tonal "function" relative to the overall organizing system. That that function is identifiable by the ear alone (and is thus a predominantly aural system), even to one unfamiliar with the piece in question, is demonstrated by the fact that one can identify "wrong notes" on the first hearing. Wrong notes in common practice tonal music are those which defy the system as a whole. One reason why the system can work is that, although the central reference point of the system, the tonic note, can be situated on any of the 12 available pitches (A, Bb, B#, C . . . G#), the system itself remains fairly stable. The term "modulation" refers to the unbroken shift from one reference point or tonic note to another within a single work or movement. The material which acts as the bridge between tonics is called the "transition section." The name of the tonal reference point is called the "key." (The tonic note is sometimes called the "key note.") Thus, the "key of C" means that the common practice system of tonality is being based on the note C—C is the tonic or key note. The key is identified in musical notation by the "key signature." There are two interrelated systems of common practice tonality called major and minor tonality which work basically the same way, but tend to produce a difference in the quality of the overall sound of the piece. Thus if a given passage written in a major key (or tonality) were altered to be played in a minor key

the essential difference would be one of "color" or feel rather than of going from order to chaos. Virtually all classical music from c. 1725-1900 uses the common practice system of tonality, and is therefore called music of the common practice period.

TONE COLOR. See timbre.

TONE ROW. See serialism.

TRIO. 1. A group of three instruments or voices or music for such a group. Piano trio refers to a piano, violin, and cello. The string trio usually consists of a violin, viola, and cello. 2. A section of the third movement of many Classical symphonies*.

TWELVE TONE. See serialism.

VARIATION, THEME AND. A form or technique of composition wherein thematic material is first introduced and then repeated numerous times, each time with some new alteration or variation. The variation technique can consist of an alteration of melody, harmony, rhythm and timbre. It is not a requisite of the form that the original material be recognizable throughout each variation, although often it is. Bach's "Goldberg Variations" and Beethoven's "Diabelli Variations" are perhaps the most famous and successful examples of the technique.

VESPERS. See Offices, the Divine.

VIOL. Also, viola da gamba. A six stringed, bowed, fretted instrument ranging in size from small enough to play on the lap to so large as to have to stand to play, with a quiet, reedy, somewhat nasal tone, popular in the Renaissance. Viol consorts ranging from groups of three to six instruments were especially popular in Renaissance England. The viol, no matter what the size, is always held in a vertical position.

VIRELAI. One of the standard forms of the Medieval and Renaissance French chanson*.

VIRGINAL. A type of harpsichord.

VOICE. The generic name for a strand of melody in a polyphonic* composition.

WORD PAINTING. A compositional technique of vocal music wherein the music overtly expresses word imagery, as when the melody goes very high on the word "mountain," and low on the word "valley." This technique played an important role in much Baroque music and in the madrigal* of the late Italian Renaissance and early Baroque.

Bibliography of Books on Music

REFERENCE WORKS
Grove's Dictionary of Music and Musicians, 5th edition, edited by Eric Blom (New York: St. Martin's Press) is the standard large (ten volume) English language music dictionary. It is terribly dated and will soon be replaced by a completely new edition. It is available in a relatively inexpensive paperback edition. *The Harvard Dictionary of Music, 2nd edition, Revised and Enlarged,* by Willi Apel (Cambridge: Belknap Press of Harvard University Press) is the best single volume music dictionary, but as it contains no articles about composers or musicians it needs to be supplemented with a separate musician's dictionary such as the standard *Baker's Biographical Dictionary of Musicians, 5th edition, Completely Revised* by Nicolas Slonimsky (New York: G. Schirmer). The *Harvard Dictionary of Music* is available in a shortened paperback edition from Pocket Books publishers. Another short, usable, inexpensive dictionary which does contain information on composers is the *New Penguin Dictionary of Music* by Arthur Jacobs (New York: Penguin Books).

music
Small inexpensive paperbound scores of much orchestral and chamber music are available in what are called "study scores" or "miniature scores." Information about these and other music can be obtained from such major music outlets as Carl Fischer, Inc. (in Los Angeles, Chicago and New York) and Broude Bros. Limited (in New York). The *Historical Anthology of Music* (HAM) by Archibald T. Davison and Willi Apel (Cambridge: Harvard University Press) is a useful anthology of pre-Classical music. W. W. Norton and Co., Inc. (in New York) also offers music anthologies.

HISTORY
GENERAL. The standard one volume history of music in English is *A History of Western Music, Revised edition,* by Donald Jay Grout (New York: W. W. Norton and Co., Inc.) Although in many ways an excellent book, the density of its over 800 pages somewhat

diminishes its attractiveness to the casual reader. (The bibliography, however, is excellent). For this reason, a shorter edition has been made available. *A Short History of Music, 4th edition, Revised* by Alfred Einstein (New York: Vintage Books), available in an expensive paperback edition, offers a reasonably good sketch outline of the history of music.

SPECIFIC PERIODS. There are three good music history series put out by W. W. Norton and Co., Inc., Prentice Hall, and Oxford University Press. The books in the Norton series vary in quality and layout, but all tend toward being long, scholarly, and somewhat dense, and demand at least minimal technical knowledge about music. The Prentice Hall series is more uniform in style and format and is directed more toward the general reader. The books in this series are shorter and tend to have less detail than those of the Norton series. Also, the Prentice Hall books are available in paperback editions. The quality and style of the Oxford series lies somewhere between the Norton and Prentice Hall books, but the high prices of these beautifully bound and printed books lessen their appeal. The bibliographies in the Norton and Oxford books are quite extensive, while those in the Prentice Hall series are shorter, but are annotated. The following is a discussion of some of the books from these series.

MEDIEVAL. Although the standard text is *Music in the Middle Ages* by Gustave Reese (Norton), it is of little value to the layman. Much of the material is very dated (Professor Reese died before completing a much needed revised edition), the level of detail is quite high, technical knowledge is assumed, and the writing style is rather stark. Norton has recently come out with another book on the same subject, *Medieval Music* by Richard Hoppin, which looks like a fine attempt at presenting a book on the subject directed toward a less specialized audience. Published separately is a useful *Anthology of Medieval Music* edited by Hoppin. Albert Seay's *Music in the Medieval World* (Prentice Hall) is a fairly short, good, accessible book.

RENAISSANCE. As with the text for Medieval music, the standard book is by Gustave Reese, *Music in the Renaissance* (Norton). Apart from being somewhat less dated, the above comments about Reese's *Music in the Middle Ages* apply here also. Another fine book, written in a clear, understandable style and aimed at the intelligent layman is Howard Brown's recent *Music in the Renaissance* (Prentice Hall).

BAROQUE. *Music in the Baroque Era* (Norton) by Manfred Bukofzer is the standard text. It is a good, well written, fairly detailed work, as is Claude Palisca's shorter *Baroque Music* (Prentice Hall).

CLASSICAL. Reinhard G. Pauly's *Music in the Classical Period* (Prentice Hall) is a short book with emphasis on historical, social, and cultural background. *The Age of Enlightenment 1745-1790* (Oxford) ed. by Egon Wellesz and Frederick Sternfield, though dealing with a shorter chronological span than Pauly's book, is considerably more thorough. This book, as with all those of the Oxford series, is the work of several scholars, each concentrating on a self-contained chapter dealing with his specialty. Charles Rosen's masterpiece, *The Classical Style* (Norton) should also be mentioned here. Although it is demanding in its terse style, its assumption of technical knowledge, and its general level of sophistication, it is one of the most intelligent and informative examples of writing about music in existence. It is not a book for beginners, but for anyone interested in the way music works, it is worth all efforts to read it.

ROMANTIC. There is no really first rate book about Romantic music. Alfred Einstein's *Music in the Romantic Era* (Norton) tends to be rather chatty, while Rey M. Longyear's *Nineteenth-Century Romanticism in Music* (Prentice Hall) is in many ways uneven.

MODERN. *Twentieth Century Music—An Introduction* (Prentice Hall) by Eric Salzman presents a clear, fairly thorough (if somewhat undiscriminating) survey of nearly all the trends in modern music. *The New Music—The Sense Behind the Sound* (New York: A Delta Book, Dell Publishing) offers an intriguing view of the background and rationale behind some of the main currents in 19th century music. Charles Rosen's short *Arnold Schoenberg* (New York: The Viking Press) is an excellent book for those interested in understanding the "problem" of 20th century music. Written with a minimum of technical jargon, the book deals with complex theoretical issues in a clear but sophisticated manner.

A NOTE ON THE MAKE-UP AND PURPOSE OF THIS GUIDE

The inclusion of composers and works in this guide, as well as their organization into homogeneous groups and hierarchic levels attempts to reflect the collective contemporary attitude toward classical music. Measures of popularity as suggested by such things as frequency of recording and performance were weighed against such academic factors as historical importance and scholarly critical evaluation to create what is hoped to be a balanced, albeit schematic view of the field.

There is a certain brand of intellectual snobbism which finds simplifying guides such as the present one distasteful. Such a narrow attitude, of course, is understandable. For snobbism, being a form of paranoia, fosters suspicion of directness. All verbal discourse is an exercise in reductionism. Indeed, that is its value. Simplification only becomes *over*-simplification when the degree of reduction is misrepresented. The *Simple Guide to Classical Music* reduces the field maximally. That is its value. The consequences of such severe reduction are those of any schematic drawing. Many, indeed all, details are left out and matters of equivocation and subtlety made one-sided and blunt. The result is a scheme or map which necessarily distorts and which is therefore highly provisional. This guid does not attempt to present a complete and rounded picture of the field of classical music. That is not its purpose. Its purpose is to help those interested discover how to gain the picture they desire.

Composers' Index